MW01178627

The God-man Living—
A Man of Prayer

Witness Lee

The Holy Word for Morning Revival

Living Stream Ministry
Anaheim, California

First Edition, June 2001.

ISBN 0-7363-1352-4

Published by

Living Stream Ministry
2431 W. La Palma Ave., Anaheim, CA 92801 U.S.A.
P. O. Box 2121, Anaheim, CA 92814 U.S.A.

Printed in the United States of America

01 02 03 04 05 06 07 / 10 9 8 7 6 5 4 3 2 1

Contents

2001 Memorial Day Weekend Conference

THE GOD-MAN LIVING— A MAN OF PRAYER

iii

Preface

1. This book is intended as an aid to believers in developing a daily time of morning revival with the Lord in His word. At the same time, it provides a review of the 2001 Memorial Day Weekend Conference on "The God-man Living—A Man of Prayer." Through intimate contact with the Lord in His word, the believers can be constituted with life and truth and thereby equipped to prophesy in the meetings of the church unto the building up of the Body of Christ.

2. The content of this book is taken primarily from the conference message outlines, the text and footnotes of the Recovery Version of the Bible, selections from the writings of Watchman Nee and Witness Lee, and *Hymns,* all of which are published by Living Stream Ministry.

3. The book is divided into weeks. One conference message is covered per week. Each week first presents the message outline, followed by six daily portions, a hymn, and then some space for writing. The message outline has been divided into days, corresponding to the six daily portions. Each daily portion covers one main point and begins with a section entitled "Morning Nourishment." This section contains selected verses and a short reading that can provide rich spiritual nourishment through intimate fellowship with the Lord. The "Morning Nourishment" is followed by a section entitled "Today's Reading," a longer portion of ministry related to the day's main point. Each day's portion concludes with a short list of references for further reading and some space for the saints to make notes concerning their spiritual inspiration, enlightenment, and enjoyment to serve as a reminder of what they have received of the Lord that day.

4. The space provided at the end of each week is for composing a short prophecy. This prophecy can be composed by considering all our daily notes, the "harvest"

of our inspirations during the week, and preparing a main point with some sub-points to be spoken in the church meetings for the organic building up of the Body of Christ.

5. The conference outlines were compiled by Living Stream Ministry from the written and spoken ministry of Watchman Nee and Witness Lee. The outlines, footnotes, and references in the Recovery Version of the Bible were written by Witness Lee. All of the other works cited in this publication were written by Watchman Nee or Witness Lee.

Memorial Day Weekend Conference

May 25-28, 2001

General Subject:

THE GOD-MAN LIVING—A MAN OF PRAYER

Banners:

Christ, the first God-man, was a man of prayer,
praying to the mysterious God
in the divine and mystical realm.

We need to copy the Lord in our spirit
by taking His yoke—God's will—
and toiling for God's economy
according to His model.

We must have some experience of prayer in private,
contacting our heavenly Father in secret,
experiencing some secret enjoyment of the Father,
and receiving some secret answer from Him.

The way to experience Christ,
to be constituted with Christ, and to live Christ
is to pray in a genuine way.

A Man of Prayer Praying to the Mysterious God in the Divine and Mystical Realm

Scripture Reading: John 10:30; 8:29; 16:32b; 14:30; 17:1; Matt. 14:23

Day 1 I. **Although in the Lord's recovery we have so much vision, every brother and sister still needs to ask the Lord for a new revival; this revival is the God-man life (Hab. 3:2a; Hosea 6:2):**

A. When we think of ourselves as God-men, this thinking, this realization, revolutionizes us in our daily experience (Gal. 2:20).

Day 2 B. The living of a God-man is the living of a man who lives God and expresses God (John 6:57; 14:9-10).

C. The Lord Jesus is the first God-man, and we are the many God-men (Rom. 8:29):

1. Christ lived a human life not by His human life but by the divine life to express the divine attributes in the human virtues (Luke 1:35; 10:25-37).

2. Because Christ is our life and our person, we should live a human life by the divine life for the expression of divinity in humanity (Col. 3:4).

3. To live the life of a God-man is to deny the self, take up the cross, and live Christ for the expression of God (Matt. 16:24; Gal. 2:20; Phil. 1:21a).

D. The divine Spirit and the human spirit are mingled within us so that we can live the life of a God-man, a life that is God yet man and man yet God (1 Cor. 6:17).

E. Eventually, the God-men will be the overcomers, the Zion within Jerusalem; this will bring in a new revival—a revival that has never occurred in history—and this will end this age (Rev. 14:1; 11:15).

Day 3
II. **The first God-man, the Lord Jesus, lived as a man of prayer (Luke 5:16):**
   A. In describing the first God-man as a man of prayer, we may use the words *divine* and *mystical; divine* is on God's side, and *mystical* is on man's side:
      1. In His living as the first God-man, all that the Lord Jesus did was divine and mystical; God was manifested in a mystical human way (1 Tim. 3:16).
      2. The Lord's mystical human life was a divine realm, and this realm is the kingdom of God (John 3:13, 3).
   B. A critical part of the history of the first God-man was His prayer (John 17):
      1. The prayers of the first God-man were in the divine and mystical realm.
      2. The Lord Jesus was a man in the flesh, yet He prayed to the mysterious God in a divine and mystical way and realm (Matt. 14:23).

Day 4
      3. His prayers were divine, yet they were in a human life, making that human life mystical (Mark 1:35; Luke 5:16; 6:12).
      4. Christ's prayers were divine facts in His mystical human life (John 17):
         a. Whatever God does is a divine fact, and in the Lord Jesus the divine facts were lived out in a human life, making His human life mystical.
         b. The Lord Jesus was a God-man, and all that He said and did were divine facts accomplished in His human life mystically (5:19).
   C. With the Lord Jesus, we see the pure pattern of the man of prayer revealed in the Gospels:
      1. As a man of prayer, the Lord Jesus was a man who was always one with God (John 10:30).
      2. As a man of prayer, the Lord Jesus was a man who lived in the presence of God without ceasing (Acts 10:38c; John 8:29; 16:32b).

3. As a man of prayer, the Lord Jesus trusted in God and not in Himself under any kind of suffering or persecution (1 Pet. 2:23b; Luke 23:46).

4. As a man of prayer, the Lord Jesus was a man in whom Satan, the ruler of the world, had nothing—no ground, no chance, no hope, and no possibility in anything; Satan had no ground in Him because His submission to the Father cut off Satan (John 14:30).

Day 5 III. **Prayer is man cooperating and co-working with God, allowing God to express Himself through man and thus accomplish His purpose (Rom. 8:26-27; James 5:17):**

A. Prayer is man breathing God, obtaining God, and being obtained by God; real prayer is an exhaling and inhaling before God, causing us and God to contact each other and to gain each other (1 Thes. 5:17).

B. A praying person cooperates with God, works together with God, and allows God to express Himself and His desire from within him and through him (Rom. 8:26-27; James 5:17; Eph. 1:17-23; 3:14-21).

C. Genuine prayers cause our being to be wholly mingled with God, causing us to pray as a man mingled with God, a God-man (Jude 20; Eph. 6:18).

Day 6 IV. **The Bible teaches us, the believers in Christ, the God-men, to live as divine and mystical persons (Matt. 28:19; 2 Cor. 13:14; Eph. 4:1-6):**

A. We have been separated from being common; we have been sanctified and separated unto God, who is holy, and now we are in the divine and mystical realm of the consummated Spirit (John 17:17, 19; Heb. 2:11; 1 Thes. 5:23).

B. Our life should be divine yet human—not merely human but mystically human; everything in our living should be divine and mystical (John 14:16-20).

C. Every believer should be a divine and mystical
person, one who is human yet lives divinely (Gal.
2:20; 2 Cor. 10:1).

D. The New Testament teaches us, the members of
the Body of Christ, to do everything with God,
in God, by God, and through God; this is what it
means to be divine (1 Cor. 10:31; Col. 3:17).

E. A genuine and proper prayer is not merely spiritual but also divine; this means that the Triune
God prays with us and that we pray by living in
the Triune God (Rom. 8:26-27; Jude 20).

F. All genuine prayers, prayers that can be
counted by God, are divine facts, something
divine performed in the mystical human life
(John 14:13-14; 16:23-24).

Morning Nourishment

Hab.   ...O Jehovah, revive Your work in the midst of the
3:2   years...
Hosea He will enliven us after two days; on the third day
6:2   He will raise us up, and we will live in His presence.
Rom.   Because those whom He foreknew, He also predesti-
8:29   nated *to be* conformed to the image of His Son, that
           He might be the Firstborn among many brothers.
Col.   When Christ our life is manifested, then you also
3:4   will be manifested with Him in glory.

In the Lord's recovery there are a few matters that are urgent
at the present time to which we should pay special attention.
First, every brother and sister needs to ask the Lord for a new
revival. Although we have so much vision, we still need to ask
the Lord for a new revival. This revival is the God-man life. In
every church, we all need to live the God-man life. Whether we
are at home or in the workplace, we all need to live the God-man
life. (*The Issue of the Union of the Consummated Spirit of the
Triune God and the Regenerated Spirit of the Believers*, p. 88)

Today's Reading

We need to understand that to be a part of mankind is to be
something negative. In God's view *mankind* is a negative term
referring to fallen man. As believers in Christ and children of
God, we are not mankind—we are God-man kind. To realize
this is to be changed, even revolutionized. When we realize that
we are God-men, we will say, "Lord, You are the first God-man,
and we are the many God-men following You. You lived a human
life, not by Your human life but by God's divine life to express
Him. His attributes became Your virtues. You were here on this
earth dying every day. You were crucified to live. Lord, You are
my life today and You are my person. You are just me. I therefore
must die. I need to be conformed to Your death. I have to be
crucified to die every day to live a God-man's life, a human life
yet not by my human life but by the divine life, with Your life

and Your nature as my constitution to express You in Your divine attributes, which become my human virtues." This makes us not just a Christian or a believer in Christ but a God-man, one kind with God. This is the highest point of God's gospel. (*Life-study of 1 & 2 Chronicles,* pp. 27-28)

We, the saved ones, are not merely forgiven of our sins; we are regenerated,...born a second time. Our first birth was of our parents, who are humans; hence, we also are humans. Today we are regenerated, born of God the Father; hence, we also are God. Our second birth was of God. Since we are born of God, surely we are the children of God. The children of God surely are God. By our first birth we became man; by our second birth we become God....We are born of God, and what is born of God surely is God. Hence, today we are not merely men but men yet God. We are children of men, and also children of God. A man has begotten me; thus, I am a man. God has begotten me; thus, I am God. By our two births we have become men yet God. This is irrefutable.

I have been stressing the fact that we are men yet God because this has too much to do with our living.... A person who is born of God should not forget his status as a son of God. If we have really seen this matter, there will always be a reminder within us: "Would a son of God speak in this way? Would he dress in this way?" No one who really recognizes that he is a son of God could ever live and act by his own desires. I can testify that when I went to a department store, each time I picked up a necktie, there was a reminder within me saying, "I am a child of God who speaks for the Lord. Can I use this tie?" Often I just put down the necktie because I knew that I could not use it. Brothers and sisters, do not forget your status....Since we are men yet God, our living should match our status. We must live the life of one who is man yet God. (*The Issue of the Union of the Consummated Spirit of the Triune God and the Regenerated Spirit of the Believers,* p. 65)

Further Reading: The Issue of the Union of the Consummated Spirit of the Triune God and the Regenerated Spirit of the Believers, chs. 5-6; Life-study of 1 & 2 Chronicles, msgs. 1-2, 4

Enlightenment and inspiration: _____

_____

Morning Nourishment

Matt. Then Jesus said to His disciples, If anyone wants
16:24 to come after Me, let him deny himself and take
up his cross and follow Me.

Gal. I am crucified with Christ; and *it is* no longer I *who*
2:20 live, but *it is* Christ *who* lives in me; and the *life*
which I now live in the flesh I live in faith, the *faith*
of the Son of God, who loved me and gave Himself
up for me.

Phil. For to me, to live is Christ...
1:21

Since we have seen such a high peak of the divine revelation, we need to put into practice what we have seen. Our practice will have a success, and that success will be a new revival—the highest revival, and probably the last revival before the Lord's coming back. As I said in the previous chapter, we need a model. I do not mean that only some individuals should become a model. I mean that we need a corporate model, a Body, a people who live the life of a God-man. From today our practice should be to live the life of a God-man by realizing the power of the resurrection of Christ to take His cross as He did, to be crucified, to be conformed to His death, every day to live another One's life (Phil. 3:10; 1:21; Gal. 2:20). Our life, our self, our flesh, our natural man, and our everything were already brought to the cross by Him. Now we are living Him, so we should remain in His crucifixion to be conformed to the mold of His death every moment in every part of our life. That will cause us to spontaneously live Him as the resurrection (John 11:25). This is the living of a God-man. (*Living a Life according to the High Peak of God's Revelation,* pp. 39-40)

Today's Reading

Let us now consider the situation in the recovery. We all are believers. We believe in the Lord Jesus. We have repented and come back to the Lord, and we have been saved, even dynamically saved. Yet in our daily life we may not have the living of a God-man.

For the children of Israel to keep the law was to live God and express God. However, they did not keep the law, and therefore they did not live God and express God. The situation is the same with us today. For the most part, we do not express God in our daily living.

We need to have a God-man living in our married life. If a married brother would live the life of a God-man in his married life, he would surely be a good husband, for he would be a real God-man in loving his wife. Likewise, if a married sister would live the life of a God-man in her married life, she would be a good wife, submitting herself to her husband.

We also need to have a God-man living in the church life, especially in relation to what we call the vital groups. How can we have a vital group if we ourselves are not vital? This is impossible. Suppose at dinner a brother and his wife are not happy with each other. They even exchange words and argue for quite a long time. Suddenly they remember that later that evening they must attend a meeting of their vital group. But how could this couple be vital in the meeting? Because they are not vital at home in their married life, they have no way to be vital in the meeting.

Because we are short of the God-man living, we need a real revival. The children of Israel had only an outward law, but today we have something much stronger and much higher than the law. We have the all-inclusive, life-giving, compounded, consummated Spirit in us, who is the bountiful supply of the Spirit of Jesus Christ (Phil. 1:19). We need to live Christ by the bountiful supply of the Spirit of Jesus Christ (vv. 20-21a).

We have such a Spirit within us, but what do we live and how do we live? Do we live Christ? In the church meetings we may live Christ, but do we live Christ at home with our husband or wife and with our children? We need a real revival to be God-men who live a life of always denying ourselves and being crucified to live Christ for the expression of God. (*Life-study of 1 & 2 Chronicles,* pp. 76-77)

Further Reading: Living a Life according to the High Peak of God's Revelation, chs. 4-5; *Life-study of 1 & 2 Chronicles,* msgs. 8, 11; *The God-man Living,* msgs. 1, 3

Enlightenment and inspiration: _____

Morning Nourishment

Luke But He Himself *often* withdrew in the wilderness
5:16 and prayed.
Matt. ...He went up to the mountain privately to pray.
14:23 And when night fell, He was there alone.
1 Tim. And confessedly, great is the mystery of godliness:
3:16 He who was manifested in the flesh...
John ...The Son can do nothing from Himself except what
5:19 He sees the Father doing, for whatever that One
does, these things the Son also does in like manner.

The Lord lived as a man of prayer. He did not live as a common man praying common prayers to God, as a pious man, a so-called godly man, praying to God in a religious way, or as a God-seeking man praying to God for the divine attainments and obtainments. His being a man of prayer was not even as merely a Christ-seeker praying desperately to gain Christ in His excellency (Phil. 3:12-14, 8). Instead, He was a man in the flesh praying to the mysterious God in the divine, mystical realm. The Gospels tell us that He often went to the mountain or withdrew to a private place to pray (Matt. 14:23; Mark 1:35; Luke 5:16; 6:12; 9:28).

In describing the first God-man as a man of prayer, I have avoided using the word *spiritual*. Instead, I have used the words *divine* and *mystical*. *Divine* is on God's side. *Mystical* is on man's side. On the one hand, Jesus was a man in the flesh, yet He prayed to the mysterious God in the divine and mystical way and realm. (*The God-man Living*, p. 89)

Today's Reading

A very critical part of the history of the first God-man was His prayer. All of His prayers were divine, yet they were in a human life, making that human life mystical. He lived a mystical human life. A husband should love his wife divinely, not merely spiritually. This is because he does not love her in his way but in God's way and not with his love but with God's love. How could a man in the flesh love his wife in a divine way and with the divine love? This is mystical. We should be persons living a life which is divine yet mystical. Our life should be divine yet human—not merely human, but mystically human. This is what is unveiled in the holy Word.

We want to continue to see the divine facts in the mystical human life of the first God-man, who was a man of prayer. His mystical human life was a divine realm, and this realm is the kingdom of God. The genuine and proper prayer should always be divine, not just spiritual. This means that the Triune God prays with us and that we pray by living with the Triune God. He is indwelling us and is one with us. The New Testament reveals clearly that the consummated Spirit, the Spirit of God as the life-giving Spirit and the Spirit of Christ, indwells us (Rom. 8:2, 9-11). Second Timothy 4:22 says that the Lord is with our spirit. The consummated God today as the compound life-giving Spirit indwells us. We are human beings, no doubt, but the divine person was added to us.

For us to be spiritual is inadequate. We have to see that God has made Himself one with us and made us one with Him. Thus, each of us believers is a God-man. In this sense, we are God in life and in nature, but of course, not in His Godhead. This is because we have been born of Him to be of His species (John 1:12-13). We are one kind with Him. Based upon this revelation, we can see that genuine prayer should be the divine expression. If we pray by ourselves, that is the human expression. If we pray by living with God and moving with Christ, we pray from this Person and our prayers are divine.

Only a divine person could pray, "Our Father who is in the heavens, Your name be sanctified" (Matt. 6:9). A divine, human person is a mystery. He is altogether mystical. There is a realm in this universe which is divine and mystical. The worldly people do not know this realm. They are in the physical, fallen, sinful, evil world. But we have been separated from being common; we have been sanctified and separated unto our God, who is holy. Now we are in the divine and mystical realm of the consummated Spirit. (*The God-man Living,* pp. 92, 98)

Further Reading: The God-man Living, msgs. 10-12

Enlightenment and inspiration: _____

_____

Morning Nourishment

John 14:30	I will no longer speak much with you, for the ruler of the world is coming, and in Me he has nothing.
17:1	These things Jesus spoke, and lifting up His eyes to heaven, He said, Father, the hour has come; glorify Your Son that the Son may glorify You.
1 Pet. 2:23	...Suffering, He did not threaten but kept committing *all* to Him who judges righteously.
Luke 23:46	And crying with a loud voice, Jesus said, Father, into Your hands I commit My spirit....

He was a man of prayer, a man who is one with God (John 10:30). We may be a Christ-seeker, desperately praying to gain Christ, yet we may not be one with God. He was also a man living in the presence of God without ceasing (Acts 10:38c; John 8:29; 16:32). He told us that He was never alone, but the Father was with Him. Every moment He saw His Father's face. We may seek Christ, yet not live in the presence of God so closely and continuously without ceasing. Also, He trusted in God and not in Himself, under any kind of suffering and persecution. First Peter 2:23b says that in the midst of His suffering He did not speak threatening words but kept committing all to Him who judges righteously. Luke 23:46 says that at the time He was dying on the cross, He prayed, "Father, into Your hands I commit My spirit." In our daily life, do we trust in God when trouble comes? Maybe we do to a small extent, but not absolutely. (*The God-man Living*, pp. 89-90)

Today's Reading

[John 14:30 tells us] that in the Lord Jesus, Satan as the ruler of the world had no ground, no chance, no hope, no possibility in anything. If we are enlightened, we will admit that Satan has too many things in us. He has the ground, the chance, the hope, and the possibility in many things. But here is a man of prayer who said that Satan, the ruler of the world, had nothing in Him. This is a particular sentence in the whole Bible. Thus, Christ was a man of prayer, a man who is one with God, lives in the presence of God continuously, trusts in God in His suffering and persecution, and in whom Satan has nothing.

All of the Lord's prayers are divine facts. We need to ask if our prayers are divine facts. A wife may ask the Lord to take care of her family because her husband has lost his job. Such a prayer is not divine. Instead, she may pray, "Lord, as a house-wife, I praise You and thank You that we are in Your hands. We trust in You in this circumstance." This is divine prayer. If we pray, "Lord, today there is a need for people to go to Moscow," this is not divine prayer. Instead, we should pray, "Lord, thank You that You are now spreading Your recovery to Russia. Lord, this is Your move." This is divine prayer.

When we consider the Lord's prayer in John 17, we can see what divine prayer is. We may pray for our need, but we have to pray about it in a divine way. We should pray divine prayers, not human prayers. All the prayers Christ prayed were divine facts in His mystical human life. Although we are human, people should sense that there is something mystical about us. Our classmates, colleagues, or peers should sense that there is something about us that they cannot understand. This is be-cause we are mysterious, mystical. The One who prayed the prayer recorded in John 17 was Jesus of Nazareth, a man in the flesh, yet His prayer was mystical.

A sister who lost her son once said she could not understand why it was that the more she loved the Lord, the more she seemed to lose. She prayed, "Lord, don't You know I love You? Why did You take away my son?" This is not only a human prayer but also a fleshly prayer. Based upon this light, we should consider our prayers. We pray many human and fleshly prayers, not divine prayers. No prayer is as high as the Lord's prayer in John 17. He prayed, "Father, the hour has come; glorify Your Son that the Son may glorify You" (v. 1). Christ's prayer is divine. When He was dying on the cross, He prayed, "Father, forgive them, for they do not know what they are doing" (Luke 23:34). He prayed to the Father for the forgiveness of His crucifiers. That was divine and mystical. (*The God-man Living,* pp. 90-91)

Further Reading: The God-man Living, msgs. 10-12

Enlightenment and inspiration: _____

_____

Morning Nourishment

Rom.   Moreover, in like manner the Spirit also joins in to
8:26-27 help *us* in our weakness, for we do not know for
        what we should pray as is fitting, but the Spirit
        Himself intercedes for *us* with groanings which
        cannot be uttered. But He who searches the hearts
        knows what the mind of the Spirit is, because He
        intercedes for the saints according to God.
James   Elijah was a man of like feeling with us, and he
5:17   earnestly prayed that it would not rain; and it did
        not rain on the earth for three years and six months.
Eph.   By means of all prayer and petition, praying at
6:18   every time in spirit...

Brothers, real prayers are the Holy Spirit within man expressing God's desire through man. In other words, real prayers are
prayers involving two parties. They are not simply man alone
praying to God, but they are the Spirit mingling with man, putting
on man, and joining with man in prayer. Outwardly it is man
praying, but inwardly it is the Spirit praying. This means two
parties express the same prayer at the same time. Please remember that this alone is the prayer which is spoken of in the Scriptures.
"Earnestly prayed" [James 5:17] in Greek means "prayed
with prayer," or "prayed in prayer." This is a very peculiar
expression in the Bible. Please remember, this is what we mean
by prayer of two parties. When Elijah was praying, he was
praying with or in a prayer. In other words, he prayed with the
prayer of the Spirit within him. Thus we can say that Elijah's
prayer was God praying to Himself in Elijah. Andrew Murray
once said that a real prayer is Christ who indwells us praying
to Christ who is sitting on the throne. That Christ would be
praying to Christ Himself sounds strange, but in our experience
this is really the case. (*Lessons on Prayer*, p. 19)

Today's Reading

Let us look again at Romans 8:27. There is a clause which
says, "The Spirit...intercedes...according to God." This means

that the Holy Spirit prays in us according to God; that is, God prays in us through His Spirit. Thus, such a prayer certainly expresses God's intention as well as God Himself.

Real prayers will certainly cause our being to be wholly mingled with God. We will become a person of two parties, i.e. God mingled with man. When you pray, it is He praying, and when He prays, it is also you praying. When He prays within you, then you express the prayer outwardly. He and you are altogether one, inside and outside; He and you both pray at the same time. At that time you and God cannot be separated, being mingled as one. Consequently, you not only cooperate with God but also work together with God that God Himself and His desire may be expressed through you, thus ultimately accomplishing God's purpose. This is the real prayer which is required of us in the Bible.

Hence, Jude verse 20 says, "Praying in the Holy Spirit." This means you should not pray in yourself....Your prayer should be the expression of two parties, you and the Holy Spirit, praying as one. Ephesians 6:18 says, "By means of all prayer and petition, praying at every time in spirit."...The spirit here does not refer solely to the Holy Spirit; rather, it also includes our human spirit. When we pray, we must pray in such a mingled spirit.

The Bible is God breathing out Himself, while prayer is our breathing in God. Bible reading and prayer are our breathing before God and thus our breathing in of God. Hence, we should not be those who only read the Bible and fail to pray. If we only read the Word, we do allow God to breathe out Himself, but we still do not breathe in God. Thus, we still need to pray. However, in our prayer our supplications for people, happenings, and things are but the outer skin, the framework. Real prayer always matches the Scriptures; it is an exhaling and inhaling before God, causing us and God, God and us, to contact one another and to obtain one another. Consequently, we wholly cooperate and work with God, and God expresses Himself and His desire through us, ultimately accomplishing His purpose. This is a fundamental meaning of prayer in the Bible. (*Lessons on Prayer,* pp. 20-21)

Further Reading: Lessons on Prayer, ch. 1

Enlightenment and inspiration: _____

Morning Nourishment

John 17:17 Sanctify them in the truth; Your word is truth.
14:13 And whatever you ask in My name, that I will do, that the Father may be glorified in the Son.
19 Yet a little while and the world beholds Me no longer, but you behold Me; because I live, you also shall live.
Jude 20 But you, beloved, building up yourselves upon your most holy faith, praying in the Holy Spirit.

We have a concept concerning spirituality which blinds us. We need to see that we should not be merely spiritual but divine and mystical. Every believer today should be a divine and a mystical person. We should be divine yet so mysterious....The key is that although we are human, we live divinely. True spirituality should make us divine. This is higher.

Sometimes when we hear a young sister giving a testimony, we have the sense that her speaking is divine yet mystical. Everything in our living should be divine and mystical. This is what we see in the Lord Jesus. When people saw what He did, they were astounded and said, "Where did this man get this wisdom and these works of power? Is not this the carpenter's son?" (Matt. 13:54-55). This is because all that He did was divine and mystical. God was living through Him. He was God manifested in the flesh. This is a great mystery. First Timothy 3:16 says that the great mystery of godliness is God manifested in the flesh. The divine is manifested in a mystical human way.

The title *God-man* indicates clearly that Jesus was a man, but He was living God. Today you are a God-man. This means that you are a man, yet you live God and express God. You are a man, yet it is God who lives in you. This is the significance of the title *God-man*. A God-man's living is a man living God. (*The God-man Living*, pp. 92-93)

Today's Reading

The New Testament teaches us, the members of the Body of Christ, to do everything with God, in God, by God, and through

God. It does not teach us to love people in an ethical way with our natural love. We have to love others by and with God, in a divine and mystical way. His love is divine, but the outward lover is a mystical human. The Bible teaches us to live as divine and mystical persons.

Now we need to consider what we should learn from the Lord's example. If we saw that a certain brother was harassed, troubled, or sick, what would we do? Perhaps we would not have the heart to care for him. On the other hand, we might care for him and want to do something for him in his need. As a result, we might hurry to see this brother and do things for him. This is our natural doing; it is not divine. Instead, we should learn of the Lord Jesus. We should go to the Lord and pray, "Lord, my brother is very sick. What would You do, Lord? Would You burden me to take care of him? If so, I will bear the burden. If not, I will not do anything by myself as a human being. I want to take care of him with You, to make this care not a human doing but a divine doing." Sometimes when we go to the Lord about a certain needy brother, He may ask us not to contact him at that time, because this brother is in His hand.

To be divine is to do everything with God, by God, in God, and through God. When someone comes to us with a burden or a problem, we should always bring it to the Lord. The Lord may say, "Leave this matter to Me. You stand aside. This is not the thing that you should do." On the other hand, if the Lord burdens us to do something, our doing will be divine.

When the Lord saw God's elect as God's flock harassed and cast away, His heart was moved with compassion. But He did not charge the disciples to directly take care of them. Instead, He told them to pray to the Lord of the harvest and ask Him to thrust out the laborers. The Lord Himself practiced this principle. He saw the need of shepherds for God's elect, so He spent the whole night in prayer to God. He did not act without prayer. He brought this case to His Father, so He got the Father's decision. (*The God-man Living*, pp. 119, 110-111)

Further Reading: The God-man Living, msgs. 10-13

Enlightenment and inspiration: _____

_____

What Miracle! What Mystery!

1 What miracle! What mystery!
  That God and man should blended be!
  God became man to make man God,
  Untraceable economy!
  From His good pleasure, heart's desire,
  His highest goal attained will be.

2 Flesh He became, the first God-man,
  His pleasure that I God may be:
  In life and nature I'm God's kind,
  Though Godhead's His exclusively.
  His attributes my virtues are;
  His glorious image shines through me.

3 No longer I alone that live,
  But God together lives with me.
  Built with the saints in the Triune God,
  His universal house we'll be,
  And His organic Body we
  For His expression corp'rately.

4 Jerusalem, the ultimate,
  Of visions the totality;
  The Triune God, tripartite man—
  A loving pair eternally—
  As man yet God they coinhere,
  A mutual dwelling place to be;
  God's glory in humanity
  Shines forth in splendor radiantly!

*Composition for prophecy with main point and
sub-points:* _____

_____

_____

_____

_____

_____

_____

_____

_____

_____

_____

_____

_____

_____

_____

_____

_____

_____

_____

_____

_____

_____

_____

_____

_____

_____

_____

_____

_____

_____

_____

_____

_____

_____

_____

_____

_____

The Pattern of Prayer
Which Is Critical to the Kingdom Life
with Four Negative Charges as Warnings

Scripture Reading: Matt. 6:5-18

Day 1 I. The example of prayer given as a pattern by the Lord increases our seeking of the kingdom of the heavens as the Father's heart's desire and affords us our need of the divine supply of grace to fulfill all the supreme and strict requirements of the kingdom of the heavens for the Father's good pleasure (Matt. 6:9-13):

A. We need to pray for the Father's name to be sanctified (v. 9):

   1. To be sanctified means to be separated and distinct from all that is common (cf. Eph. 1:4).

   2. For His name to be sanctified we should express Him in our living with a sanctified life, a daily life separated from being common and saturated with His holy nature (1 Pet. 4:15-16; Eph. 5:26; Heb. 12:10; 2 Pet. 1:4; cf. Ezek. 36:21).

Day 2 B. We need to pray for the Father's heavenly kingdom to come (Matt. 6:10):

   1. Before his fall, Satan as the archangel was appointed by God to be the ruler of the world (Ezek. 28:13-14); hence, he is called the ruler of this world (John 12:31) and holds all the kingdoms of this world and their glory in his hand (Luke 4:6).

   2. In order for God's kingdom to come in its manifestation, we must live in the reality of His kingdom today, allowing Christ as the life-giving Spirit to rule within us so that we may have righteousness, peace, and joy in the Holy Spirit (Rom. 14:17).

C. We need to pray for the Father's divine will to be done on earth (Matt. 6:10):

1. For the divine will to be done on earth is to bring the heavenly ruling, the kingdom of the heavens, to this earth (cf. Matt. 8:9a; Rom. 5:17).

2. The will of God is to have Christ as the replacement for all the offerings in the Old Testament so that we may enjoy Him as everything in living and practicing the Body life for the building up of the Body of Christ as the organism of the Triune God (Heb. 10:5-10; Rom. 12:2; Eph. 1:5, 9-11).

Day 3   D. This prayer as a pattern cares first for God's name, God's kingdom, and God's will, and second, for our need (Matt. 6:11):

1. These three things—the name, the kingdom, and the will—are the attributes of the one Triune God:

   a. The name is of the Father, because the Father is the source; the kingdom is of the Son, and the will is of the Spirit.

   b. To pray in this way is to pray that the Triune God will be prevailing on the earth as He is prevailing in the heavens.

2. The Lord as our King does not want His people to worry about tomorrow (v. 34); He wants them to pray only for today's needs, for their daily bread, which indicates a living that is by faith.

3. The kingdom people should not live on what they have stored; rather, they should live, by faith, on the Father's supply.

E. In this prayer as a pattern, we need to take care of our failures before God and of our relationship with others, asking the Father to forgive us our debts, as we also have forgiven our debtors (v. 12).

Day 4

F. This prayer as a pattern cares for the kingdom people's deliverance from the evil one and from evil things (v. 13a):

1. The kingdom people should ask the Father not to bring them into temptation but to deliver them from the evil one, the devil, and from the evil that is out of him (cf. Eph. 5:15-18).

2. To ask the Lord not to bring us into temptation indicates our knowledge of our weakness (cf. Matt. 26:41; 1 Cor. 10:13).

G. This prayer as a pattern concludes with the kingdom people's recognizing and praising reverently that the kingdom, the power, and the glory belong to the Father forever (Matt. 6:13b):

1. The kingdom is of the Son, which is the realm in which God exercises His power; the power is of the Spirit, which carries out God's intention so that the Father can express His glory (cf. 12:28).

2. This indicates that the prayer which the Lord teaches us to pray begins with the Triune God, in the sequence of the Father, the Son, and the Spirit, and ends also with the Triune God, but in the sequence of the Son, the Spirit, and the Father.

3. Thus, the prayer taught by the Lord in His supreme teaching begins with God the Father and ends also with God the Father; God the Father is both the beginning and the end, the Alpha and the Omega (cf. Eph. 4:6; 1 Cor. 15:28).

Day 5

II. **Along with this pattern of prayer, the Lord gives us four negative charges as warnings (Matt. 6:5-8, 14-18):**

A. We should not pray as the hypocrites do, loving to make a show publicly that they may be seen by and receive glory from men according to the lust of their fleshly desire; we should enter into our private room, shutting our door and praying to the Father in the heavens to be seen by Him in secret and be repaid by Him (vv. 5-6).

B. We should not pray as the Gentiles do, babbling empty words, supposing that in our multiplicity of words we will be heard; we should not be like them, for our Father knows the things that we need before we ask Him (vv. 7-8).

Day 6

C. If we forgive men's offenses, our heavenly Father will forgive us also; otherwise, our Father will not forgive our offenses, and our prayer to our heavenly Father will be annulled (vv. 14-15; cf. 18:21-35).

D. We should not fast like the sullen-faced hypocrites, disfiguring our faces so that our fast may appear to men; instead, we should fast by anointing our head and washing our face that our fast may not appear to men but to our Father who is in secret, who sees in secret, and who will repay us (6:16-18).

Morning Nourishment

Matt. You then pray in this way: Our Father who is in
6:9 the heavens, Your name be sanctified.
Acts So they went from the presence of the Sanhedrin,
5:41 rejoicing that they were counted worthy to be
dishonored on behalf of the Name.
Heb. ...[God disciplines] for what is profitable that we
12:10 might partake of His holiness.

To be sanctified means to be separated and distinct from all
that is common. On the fallen earth there are many false gods.
The worldly people consider our God as being in common with
those gods. If we pray for our Father's name to be sanctified, we
should not just utter this with our words. For His name to be
sanctified, we should express Him in our living. We must live a
sanctified life, a daily life separated from being common. To pray
such a prayer needs us to be sanctified persons, those who are
separated from being common. We should be distinct, separate,
from all of the people around us. In other words, we should be
holy. As sanctified people, we should pray, "Our Father, Your
name be sanctified." (*The God-man Living,* pp. 99-100)

Today's Reading

"Your name be sanctified!" God has an expectation that we all
pray for His name to be sanctified by men. His name is exalted
among the angels. But on earth, His name is being used in vain;
even the idols use His name. When a man takes the name of
God in vain, God does not show His wrath by striking him with
thunder. He hides Himself, as if He did not exist. When a man
takes His name in vain, He does not do anything to deal with
him. Yet He wants His children to pray, "Your name be sanctified."...If you love God and know Him, you will want His name
to be sanctified. If anyone takes God's name in vain, you will
feel hurt, your desire will be even stronger, and you will pray
even more earnestly: "Your name be sanctified." One day man
will sanctify this name and no longer take this name in vain.

"Your name be sanctified!" God's name is not only a title we address with our mouth; it is a great revelation we receive from the Lord. God's name is used in the Bible to designate His revelation to man concerning Himself; it denotes everything we know about Him. God's name speaks of God's nature, and it reveals His fullness. This is not something that man can understand with his soul but something that the Lord reveals to us (John 17:6). The Lord said, "And I have made Your name known to them and will yet make it known, that the love with which You have loved Me may be in them, and I in them" (17:26). This shows us that in order to know God's name, we need the Lord to make it known to us again and again.

"Your name be sanctified!" This is not only our desire but also our worship to the Father. We should give glory to God. We should begin our prayer with praises. Before we can hope to receive mercy and grace from Him, we should give glory to Him. We should allow Him to gain the fullest praise concerning Himself, and then we should receive grace from Him. Brothers and sisters, we have to remember that the main thing and the ultimate goal in our prayer is for God to gain glory.

"Your name be sanctified!" God's name is linked to God's glory. Ezekiel 36 says, "But I had regard for My holy name, which the house of Israel had profaned among the nations, where they went" (v. 21). This means that the house of Israel had not sanctified God's name, so God's name was profaned wherever they went among the nations. Yet God had regard for His holy name. Our Lord wants us to have this desire. In other words, He wants to glorify His own name through us. God's name must first be sanctified in our hearts before our desire can be turned to something more profound. There must be a deep work of the cross before we can glorify God's name. Otherwise, our desire is not even a desire but only an empty idea. Brothers and sisters, this being the case, how much we need to be dealt with and trimmed. (Watchman Nee, *The Prayer Ministry of the Church,* pp. 32-33)

Further Reading: The God-man Living, msg. 11; *The Prayer Ministry of the Church,* ch. 2; *Life-study of Matthew,* msg. 21

Enlightenment and inspiration: _____

_____

Morning Nourishment

Matt. Your kingdom come; Your will be done, as in
6:10 heaven, *so* also on earth.
Rom. For the kingdom of God is not eating and drink-
14:17 ing, but righteousness and peace and joy in the
Holy Spirit.

Today the world is not God's kingdom but His enemy's
kingdom. This is why the Bible says that Satan is the ruler of
today's world (John 12:31). In Satan's kingdom, the world, there
is no righteousness, no peace, and no joy. Romans 14:17 tells
us that the reality of the kingdom life is righteousness, peace,
and joy in the Holy Spirit. In Satan's kingdom today, there is
no joy, because there is no peace. In the United Nations, peace
is talked about all the time, but there is no peace, because there
is no righteousness. Peace is the issue of righteousness. In his
second Epistle, Peter tells us that the unique thing that dwells
in the new heavens and new earth is righteousness (3:13). In
the coming kingdom, the millennium, the primary thing will
be righteousness. There is no righteousness in today's world,
because this is the kingdom of Satan, the evil ruler.
      Today Satan's will is being done on the earth through evil
men....Thank the Lord that Satan's will is not fully carried out.
Hitler, Mussolini, and Stalin were destroyed. Napoleon wanted
his will to be done, but he did not succeed. We need to pray for
the Father's divine will to be done on earth as in the heavens.
This is to bring the heavenly ruling, the kingdom of the
heavens, to this earth. Then the Father's will surely will be
done on the earth. (*The God-man Living,* p. 100)

Today's Reading

      The Lord teaches us to pray, "Your kingdom come." This
means that the kingdom of God is in heaven, but the kingdom
of God is not on earth. Consequently, we have to pray for God
to expand the heavenly sphere to the earth....The Lord said,
"If I, by the Spirit of God, cast out the demons, then the kingdom
of God has come upon you" (Matt. 12:28)....The kingdom of God

is wherever the Son of God casts out demons....In the Old Testament, one only finds prophecy concerning the kingdom of the heavens. When the Lord Jesus came, we had the declaration of John the Baptist, who proclaimed that the kingdom of the heavens had drawn near (Matt. 3:1-2). Then the Lord Jesus Himself said that the kingdom of the heavens had drawn near (4:17). They said this because by then there were people who were already of the kingdom of the heavens. By Matthew 13, we have the appearance of the kingdom of the heavens on earth. Today the kingdom of God is wherever God's children cast the demons and their works out by the Spirit of God. In asking us to pray for His kingdom to come, the Lord is looking forward to the time when God's kingdom will fill the whole earth.

"Your kingdom come!" This is not only a desire of the church, but also a responsibility of the church. The church should bring in God's kingdom. In order to bring in God's kingdom, the church has to pay the price to be restricted by heaven and come under heaven's rule. It has to be the outlet for heaven, and it has to allow heaven's authority to be expressed on earth. In order to bring in God's kingdom, the church has to know all the schemes of Satan (2 Cor. 2:11). It has to put on the whole armor of God and stand against the stratagems of the devil (Eph. 6:11), for wherever the kingdom of God is, the devil is cast out. When the kingdom of God rules on earth fully, Satan will be cast into the abyss (Rev. 20:1-3). Since the church has such a tremendous responsibility, Satan will do all he can to attack the church. May the church pray like the saints of old, "O Jehovah, bow Your heavens down and descend" (Psa. 144:5). "Oh that You would rend the heavens, that You would come down" (Isa. 64:1). At the same time, we should say to Satan, "Depart from the earth immediately, and go to the eternal fire which God has prepared for you" (cf. Matt. 25:41). (Watchman Nee, *The Prayer Ministry of the Church,* pp. 34-35)

Further Reading: The God-man Living, msg. 11; *The Prayer Ministry of the Church,* ch. 2; *Life-study of Matthew,* msg. 21

Enlightenment and inspiration: _____

_____

_____

Morning Nourishment

Matt. Give us today our daily bread. And forgive us our
6:11-12 debts, as we also have forgiven our debtors.
   34 Therefore do not be anxious for tomorrow, for
        tomorrow will be anxious for itself; sufficient for
        the day is its *own* evil.

In His prayer, the Lord covers our daily necessity. He teaches us to pray for our bread only for one day. We are to ask our Father to give us today, not tomorrow or next month, our daily bread. He does not want His people to worry about tomorrow. He wants them to pray only for today's needs. When I was younger, we co-workers in China sometimes came to the end of our material supply, and we did not know how we would live the next day. Something always came to meet our need for that day. The Lord is faithful to take care of the supply of our daily necessity.

In the Lord's prayer, we see that we need to take care of our relationship with others. As we ask the Father to forgive us our debts, we should forgive our debtors. We are in debt with God, and we also have debtors who owe us something. To maintain a peaceful relationship with others, we have to forgive them. Thus, we have to clear up any separating factors between us and God and between us and others. (*The God-man Living,* p. 101)

Today's Reading

This prayer also shows us that we have to look to God and pray to Him every day. The Lord teaches us to pray: "Give us *today* our daily bread." We do not pray weekly, but daily. On earth we have no support, and we have no savings. To some extent we cannot pray for weekly bread or monthly bread; we have to pray for bread *today.* How much trust in God is required here! The Lord is not ignorant of our daily needs; He does not tell us to forget about praying for these needs. Rather, He tells us to pray daily. Actually, the Father already knows the things that we need. The Lord wants us to ask God for our bread day by day because He wants us to learn to look to the Father day by day; He wants us to exercise our faith day by day. We often extend our worries too much into the future, and we stretch our prayer too much into the future. Brothers and sisters, if we have a strong desire to be for His name, His kingdom, and His will, we will suffer great hardships. But if God will give us our daily bread, we will not have to pray for tomorrow's bread until tomorrow comes. Brothers and sisters, do not worry about tomorrow; sufficient for the day is its own evil (Matt. 6:31-34).

We have to ask God to forgive our debts as we have forgiven our debtors. If a person is mean toward other brothers and sisters and does not forget their offenses against him, he cannot ask God to forgive his debts. A narrow-minded person, who always pays attention to how others have offended, hurt, or ill-treated him, cannot pray such a prayer before God. A man must have a forgiving heart before he can boldly ask the Father: "Forgive us our debts, as we also have forgiven our debtors."

Here we have to pay attention to one thing: The Bible tells us not only about our relationship with the Father but also about our relationship with one another as brothers and sisters. If a brother only remembers his relationship with God and forgets his relationship with other brothers and sisters and presumes that there is nothing wrong between him and God, he is deceiving himself....Never overlook your relationship with the brothers and sisters. If there is a barrier between you and another brother or sister, you will immediately lose God's blessing....If we have not forgiven our debtors, our debts will be remembered before God. If we have removed from our heart their debt and there is nothing there anymore, we can come boldly before God and say, "Forgive us our debts, as we also have forgiven our debtors." God will have to forgive us. Brothers and sisters, we must thoroughly forgive our debtors. Otherwise, it will affect our being forgiven before God. (Watchman Nee, *The Prayer Ministry of the Church*, pp. 38-39, 40-41)

Further Reading: The God-man Living, msg. 11; *The Prayer Ministry of the Church*, ch. 2; *Life-study of Matthew*, msg. 21

Enlightenment and inspiration: _____

_____

_____

_____

Morning Nourishment

Matt. **And do not bring us into temptation, but deliver**
6:13 **us from the evil one....**
26:41 **Watch and pray that you may not enter into**
temptation....
Eph. **Redeeming the time, because the days are evil.**
5:16

The patterned prayer cares for the kingdom people in
dealing with the evil one. They should ask the Father not to
bring them into temptation, but to deliver them from the evil
one, Satan, the devil [Matt. 6:13]. Remember, the King was led
into temptation....Sometimes the Father brings us into a situation where we are tried and tempted. Thus, as we pray to the
Father, we must recognize our weakness and say, "Father, I am
very weak. Do not bring me into temptation." This implies that
you admit that you are weak. If you do not recognize your
weakness, you will probably not pray in this manner. Rather,
you may feel that you are strong. That will be the very time
the Father will bring you into temptation to show you that you
are not strong at all. Thus, it is better for our prayer to indicate
to the Father that we know our weakness. We should say,
"Father, I fully realize that I am weak. Please do not bring me
into temptation. There is no need for You to do that, Father, for
I recognize my weakness." Never say to yourself, "Whatever
happens, I am confident I can stand." If that is your attitude,
be prepared to be led into the wilderness to confront temptation. Instead of having such an attitude, pray that the Father
would not bring you into temptation, but that He would deliver
you from the evil one. (*Life-study of Matthew,* pp. 268-269)

Today's Reading

[In Matthew 6:11-13a], the first part speaks of our material
needs. The second part speaks of our relationship with the
brothers and sisters. This part speaks of our relationship with
Satan. "Do not bring us into temptation." This is the negative
request. "But deliver us from the evil one." This is the positive
request. On the one hand, when we live for God on earth and

have a strong desire to be for His name, His kingdom, and His will, we have material needs; we need to ask for our daily bread. On the other hand, our conscience needs to be clean and void of offense before God; we need God to forgive our debts. But there is another thing. We also need peace; we need to ask God to deliver us from the hands of Satan. Brothers and sisters, the more we take the way of the kingdom of the heavens, the greater the temptations will be. What then should we do? We can pray and ask God not to "bring us into temptation." Brothers and sisters, we cannot be so confident in ourselves that we can scorn any temptation. Since the Lord has asked us to pray, we should pray that God would not bring us into temptation. We do not know when temptation will come. But we can pray ahead of time that we not be brought into temptation. This prayer is for our protection.

Not only do we have to ask God not to bring us into temptation, but we also have to ask Him to "deliver us from the evil one." This is a positive prayer. No matter where Satan puts his hand, we have to ask the Lord to deliver us from the evil one. In our daily bread, in the matter of condemnation in our conscience, and in any temptation, we have to ask the Lord to deliver us from the evil one. In other words, we pray that we not fall into the hand of the evil one in anything. In reading Matthew 8 and 9, we find that Satan's hands are beyond what we expect and know. They are hidden behind the fever which comes suddenly upon a person's body (8:14) and the storm which rises suddenly from the sea (8:24). They cause the demons to attach themselves to men and drown the pigs (8:28-32). They work within man's heart and cause him to reject and oppose the Lord for no reason at all (9:3, 11). In short, Satan is out to harm man and inflict suffering on man. Therefore, we have to pray that we will be delivered from the evil one. (Watchman Nee, *The Prayer Ministry of the Church*, pp. 41-43)

Further Reading: The God-man Living, msg. 11; The Prayer Ministry of the Church, ch. 2; Life-study of Matthew, msg. 21

Enlightenment and inspiration: _____

_____

_____

Morning Nourishment

Matt. And when you pray, you shall not be like the
6:5-6 hypocrites, because they love to pray standing in
the synagogues and on the street corners, so that
they may be seen by men. Truly I say to you, They
have their reward in full. But you, when you pray,
enter into your private room, and shut your door
and pray to your Father who is in secret; and your
Father who sees in secret will repay you.

The Lord warned His disciples not to pray as the hypocrites
do with a mask. They love to make a show publicly that they
may be seen by men and receive glory from them according to
the lust of their fleshly desire. Instead, the disciples should
enter into their private room, shutting their door and praying
to the Father in the heavens to be seen by Him in secret and
repaid by Him (Matt. 6:5-6). We have to learn to be secret persons.
We should pray in our private place to be seen by the Father
in secret, not by others for an outward public display. If we pray
properly, God will repay us as a reward. The hypocrites have
received their reward already, but we want to receive our God's
repayment. (*The God-man Living*, pp. 102-103)

Today's Reading

Prayer is for the purpose of fellowshipping with God and
expressing His glory. But hypocrites utilize prayers that are
for the glorification of God to glorify themselves. Consequently,
they like to pray in the synagogues and on the street corners.
They do this in order to be seen by others, because synagogues
and street corners are public places, places that men pass by
all the time. They do not pray in order to be heard by God but
to be heard by men. They want to show themselves off. This
kind of prayer is very superficial; it cannot be considered as a
prayer to God, and it cannot be considered as fellowship with
God. These men cannot expect to receive anything from God,
because the motive behind this kind of prayer is to receive glory
from men, and because there is no supply reserved before God.

They have already received their reward; they have received men's praise. Therefore, in the future kingdom, there will be nothing to remember.

What then should we do when we pray? The Lord said, "...Enter into your private room...." The private room here is a symbol. The synagogues and street corners both refer to open places, while the private room refers to a hidden place. Brothers and sisters, you can find the private room in the synagogues and on the street corners. You can find the private room on the sidewalk and in a car. The private room is the place where you fellowship with God in secret; it is the place where you pray without trying consciously to exhibit your prayer. "Enter into your private room, and shut your door." This means to shut out the world and shut yourself in. In other words, it is to ignore all the outside voices and to pray to God quietly and alone.

When you "pray to your Father who is in secret...your Father who sees in secret will repay you." What a great comfort this is! In order to pray to the Father who is in secret, you need to have faith. Although you do not feel anything outwardly, you have to believe that you are praying to the Father who is in secret! He is in secret, in a place that human eyes cannot see. Yet He is truly there. He does not despise your prayer; He sees you. This shows how much He cares for your prayers. He does not see you and then leave; He will repay you. Brothers and sisters, can you believe this word? If the Lord said that He will repay you, it means that He will repay you. The Lord guarantees that your prayer in secret will not be in vain. If you pray in a proper way, the Father will repay you. Even if there does not appear to be any repayment today, there will be repayment one day. Brothers and sisters, does your prayer in secret pass the test of the Father's seeing in secret? Do you believe that the Father sees you in secret and will repay you? (Watchman Nee, *The Prayer Ministry of the Church,* pp. 28-29)

Further Reading: The God-man Living, msg. 11; *The Prayer Ministry of the Church,* ch. 2; *Life-study of Matthew,* msg. 21

Enlightenment and inspiration: _____

_____

_____

Morning Nourishment

Matt. For if you forgive men their offenses, your heav-
6:14-18 enly Father will forgive you also; but if you do not
forgive men their offenses, neither will your Father forgive your offenses. And when you fast, do
not be like the sullen-faced hypocrites, for they
disfigure their faces so that they may appear to
men to be fasting. Truly I say to you, They have
their reward in full. But you, when you fast, anoint
your head and wash your face, so that you may not
appear to men to be fasting, but to your Father
who is in secret; and your Father who sees in
secret will repay you.

[Matthew 6:14] is the Lord's interpretation of verse 12,
which says, "Forgive us our debts, as we also have forgiven our
debtors." It is easy for Christians to fail in the matter of
forgiving others. If any unforgivingness exists among God's
children, all lessons, faith, and power will leak away. This is
why the Lord is so strong and clear. This is a simple word. Yet
God's children need this simple word. "For if you forgive men
their offenses, your heavenly Father will forgive you also." It is
so simple for us to receive the Father's forgiveness. However,
"if you do not forgive men their offenses, neither will your
Father forgive your offenses." There is no such thing as careless
forgiveness. This word is simple, but the fact is not that simple.
If we forgive others with our mouth but do not forgive in our
heart, it is not considered as forgiveness in the Father's eyes.
Forgiveness which is in the mouth only is vain and deceitful
and does not count before the Father. We must forgive others'
offenses from the heart. Just as the disciples needed this word
of the Lord, we also need the same word. (Watchman Nee, *The
Prayer Ministry of the Church*, p. 45)

Today's Reading

If Christians are irreconcilable and if they do not forgive
others from their heart, the church will run into problems. If

we have no intention of behaving like the church and if we want
to each take our own way as soon as we disagree with a single
word, we do not need to forgive one another. But the Lord
knows how crucial this matter is to us. Therefore, He reempha-
sized it at the end of the prayer. The Lord knows that the more
we communicate and fellowship with one another, the more we
need to forgive one another. He knows how crucial this matter
is. Therefore, He had to turn our attention to it. If we do not
forgive one another, it will be easy for us to give place to the
devil. If we cannot forgive one another, we are not people of the
kingdom, and we cannot do the work of the kingdom. No one
who is unforgiving can be in the work of the kingdom, and no
one who is unforgiving can be a person in the kingdom. Whenever we develop a problem with the brothers and sisters, we
develop a problem with the Lord. We cannot pray to the Lord
on the one hand and remain unforgiving on the other hand.
Brothers and sisters, this is not an insignificant thing. We must
pay attention to what the Lord pays attention to. We must
forgive others their offenses. (Watchman Nee, *The Prayer
Ministry of the Church,* pp. 45-46)

In Matthew 6:16 through 18 the King speaks regarding
fasting. Instead of appearing to men to fast, we should fast in
secret....To fast is not to refrain from eating; it is being unable
to eat because of being desperately burdened to pray for certain
things. It is also an expression of self-humbling in seeking
mercy of God. To give alms is to give what we have the right to
possess, whereas to fast is to give up what we have the right
to enjoy. Verses 17 and 18 say, "But you, when you fast, anoint
your head and wash your face, so that you may not appear to
men to be fasting, but to your Father who is in secret; and your
Father who sees in secret will repay you." This indicates that
our fasting, like our giving of alms and praying, must be done
in secret, not before men. The Father sees in secret, and He will
repay us. (*Life-study of Matthew,* p. 270)

Further Reading: The God-man Living, msg. 11; *The Prayer
Ministry of the Church,* ch. 2; *Life-study of Matthew,* msg. 21

Enlightenment and inspiration: _____

_____

Hymns, #793

1 My soul, be silent, wait upon the Lord!
   First let Him speak to thee, then speak to Him;
   True prayer in thee the Lord initiates,
   Thou but a channel art expressing Him.

2 My soul, be silent, wait upon the Lord!
   Learn to deny thy thought and all thy will.
   Learn to let God anoint thee with Himself
   And thru thy prayer His purposes fulfill.

3 My soul, be silent, wait upon the Lord!
   Silent to all thy wishes and thy plans,
   Silent to all thy earthly cares and calls,
   That God may work in thee all His demands.

4 My soul, be silent, wait upon the Lord!
   Yield to the spirit all thy heart and mind;
   Here let the spirit show what God reveals,
   Thee its obedient servant thus to find.

5 My soul, be silent, wait upon the Lord!
   Learn thus to let the Spirit pray thru thee;
   All of thy being with the Spirit move,
   Thy prayer will thus God's own expression be.

6 My soul, be silent, wait upon the Lord!
   Till in the spirit thou with God art one,
   Till thru the spirit God possesses all
   And thus transforms each part unto His Son.

7 My soul, be silent, wait upon the Lord!
   Till God may freely, fully flow thru thee,
   Till all thy words and actions hour by hour
   Are the fulfillment of God's will thru thee.

Composition for prophecy with main point and sub-points: _____

_____

_____

_____

_____

_____

_____

_____

_____

_____

_____

_____

_____

_____

_____

_____

_____

_____

_____

_____

_____

_____

_____

_____

_____

_____

_____

_____

_____

_____

_____

_____

_____

_____

The First God-man's Surpassing Prayer to His Father and His Unveiling Teaching to His Followers in Matthew 11:25-30

Scripture Reading: Matt. 11:25-30

Day 1

I. The first God-man, after reproaching the surrounding cities for not being willing to receive His teaching and repent (Matt. 11:20-24), prayed to the Father (vv. 25-26):

A. In His prayer the Lord extolled the Father, acknowledging the Father as Lord of heaven and of earth:

1. Although people, instead of responding to His ministry, slandered Him (vv. 16-19) and the leading cities rejected Him (vv. 20-24), He extolled the Father, acknowledging the Father's will:

a. While the Lord was rebuking the cities, He fellowshipped with the Father; at that time, He answered the Father, speaking to Him the extolment (vv. 25-26).

b. He did not seek prosperity in His work but sought the Father's will.

c. His satisfaction and rest were not in being understood and welcomed by man but in being known by the Father (vv. 26-27).

Day 2

2. In the Lord's extolling address, *Father* refers to the Father's relationship with Him, the Son, whereas *Lord of heaven and of earth* refers to God's relationship with the universe:

a. When God's people were defeated by His enemy, God was called "the God of heaven" (Ezra 5:12; Dan. 2:18, 37); but because Abraham was a man on the earth standing for God, he called God the "Possessor of heaven and earth" (Gen. 14:19, 22).

b. The Lord as the Son of Man called the Father "Lord of heaven and of earth," indicating that He was standing on the earth for God's interest.

B. The Lord praised the Father that He has hidden all the things mentioned in Matthew 11:27 (the knowledge of the Son and of the Father) from the wise and intelligent and has revealed them to infants:

1. *The wise and intelligent* refers to all the peoples in the cities who rejected the Lord and who were wise and intelligent in their own eyes.

2. The Father's will was to hide the knowledge of the Son and of the Father from such people and reveal it to the disciples, who are the infants (Matt. 19:13-14; 1 Cor. 1:26-28).

Day 3 II. **Based upon His prayer, He gave an unveiling teaching to His disciples (Matt. 11:27-30):**

A. The Lord's teaching is regarding the eternal economy of God (Matt. 11:27):

1. The Father has delivered all His elect to the Son for the building up of the Son's Body (v. 27a; John 6:37, 44, 65; 17:6b; 18:9).

2. Only the Father knows the Son as the centrality and universality of His economy (Matt. 11:27b; cf. Col. 2:2; Matt. 16:15-17; Gal. 1:15-16; Eph. 3:4; Phil. 3:10):

Day 4   a. The economy of the Triune God is for Him to dispense Himself into His chosen and redeemed people to make them His expression (1 Tim. 1:4).

b. Christ is the hub, the rim, and the spokes—the entire content—of God's economy (Col. 1:17-18; 3:10-11).

c. The New Testament reveals Christ in the flesh in the Gospels (John 1:14), Christ as the life-giving Spirit in the Epistles

(1 Cor. 15:45b), and Christ as the sevenfold intensified life-giving Spirit in
Revelation (Rev. 1:4; 3:1; 4:5; 5:6).

  d. For us to know the Son, the Father must
  reveal Him to us (Matt. 16:17; Eph. 1:17).

  e. We should aspire, like Paul, to know the
  all-inclusive, all-extensive, and unlimited
  Christ (Phil. 3:8-10).

3. Only the Son knows the Father as the source
and Maker of His economy (Matt. 11:27c):

  a. No one fully knows the Father except the
  Son and those believers to whom the Son
  wills to reveal the Father.

  b. For us to know the Father, the Son must
  reveal Him to us (John 17:6, 26; cf. 14:8-
  10).

4. The Son reveals the Father to His believers
for the formation of His Body (Matt. 11:27d;
John 17:6a):

  a. God's economy is for the expression of the
  Father through the Son with His organism, the Body of Christ.

  b. The Father as the source has a desire to
  have an organism through the Son, and
  the Son came to call God's elect to come to
  Him so that He can regenerate, sanctify,
  and transform them, making them His
  Body to be the organism of the Triune
  God.

Day 5 B. The Lord's teaching is regarding Himself, the
first God-man, as the Head of the Body, the
prototype, and the model (Matt. 11:28-30; Col.
1:18a; John 12:24; 1 Pet. 2:21):

1. He was absolutely submissive to God and
altogether satisfied with God (Matt. 11:26;
26:39, 42).

2. He was meek, not resisting the opponents,
and lowly, humbling Himself among men in
His heart (11:29).

C. The Lord's teaching is regarding His believers as the members of His Body, His reproduction, and His duplication:

1. The Lord's believers answer His call in their heart and come to Him bodily, with their entire being (v. 28a; Rom. 12:1).

2. The believers copy the Lord in their spirit by taking His yoke—God's will—and toiling for God's economy according to His model (Matt. 11:29a; 1 Pet. 2:21).

3. The rest that we find by taking the Lord's yoke and learning from Him is for our soul; we share in our soul His rest in satisfaction (Matt. 11:28b, 29b, 30).

4. The Lord's yoke (the Father's will) is easy, not bitter, and His burden (the work of carrying out the Father's will) is light, not heavy (v. 30).

Morning Nourishment

Matt. At that time Jesus answered and said, I extol You,
11:25-27 Father, Lord of heaven and of earth, because You
have hidden these things from the wise and intelligent and have revealed them to infants. Yes,
Father, for thus it has been well-pleasing in Your
sight. All things have been delivered to Me by My
Father, and no one fully knows the Son except the
Father; neither does anyone fully know the Father
except the Son and him to whom the Son wills to
reveal *Him.*

The first God-man, after reproaching the surrounding cities
for not being willing to receive His teaching and repent (Matt.
11:20-24), prayed to the Father, and based upon His prayer, He
gave a wonderful teaching to His disciples (vv. 25-30). Most of
the time, we cannot pray after reproaching people. If a father
cannot pray after reproaching his children, his reproaching
was not divine. But if we can still pray after reproaching
someone, our reproaching was divine.

While the first God-man was rebuking the cities, He fellowshipped with the Father, answering the Father by His prayer.
The Lord's prayer was actually His answering the Father. That
indicates that while He was reproaching, He was fellowshipping with the Father. When a father reproaches his children,
he should remain in fellowship with the Lord. (*The God-man
Living,* p. 111)

Today's Reading

As the Lord was rebuking the cities, a third party was
present. The Lord was the first party, the cities were the second
party, and the Father, who was with Him, was the third party.
As the Lord was rebuking Chorazin, Bethsaida, and Caper-
naum, the Father might have asked Him, "Are you happy about
this?" Then the Lord answered and said, "I extol You, Father."
The Father might have said to the Son, "You are rebuking these
cities because they have rejected You. Do You feel good about

this?" The Lord immediately answered and praised the Father, the Lord of heaven and earth.

Sometimes a third party is present when you are talking to your wife. You are the first party, your wife is the second party, and the Lord is the third party. Perhaps you say to your wife, "Yesterday, you did not treat me very well; your behavior was poor." As you are saying these words, the third party standing by may ask, "How about it? Do you like it? Yes, your wife was not so good yesterday." At such a time could you say, "I extol You, Father"? This is not an easy thing for us to do. But the Lord Jesus could do it, saying, "I extol You, Father, Lord of heaven and of earth. I recognize Your authority. If this were not of You, none of these cities would reject Me. Even their rejection is of You. Father, I take sides with You. This situation is quite good. I tell You that I feel good about it, and I can praise You for it."

The Greek word rendered extol in verse 25 means to make acknowledgment with praise. The Lord acknowledged the Father's way in carrying out His economy with praise. Although people, instead of responding to His ministry, slandered Him (vv. 16-19), and the leading cities rejected Him (vv. 20-24), He praised the Father, acknowledging the Father's will. He did not seek prosperity in His work, but He sought the Father's will. He would be satisfied and rest, not in man's understanding and welcome, but in the Father's knowing (vv. 26-27). Christ believed that the cities' rejection of Him was of the Father. What about our situation today? When we are rejected, opposed, criticized, attacked, and condemned, could we praise the Father? Have you ever said, "Father, I praise You for the rejection and opposition of my parents and friends"? We need to recognize that such rejection is sovereignly of the Lord and praise Him for it. (*Life-study of Matthew*, pp. 386-387)

Further Reading: The God-man Living, msg. 12; *Life-study of Matthew*, msg. 31

Enlightenment and inspiration: _____

_____

_____

_____

Morning Nourishment

1 Cor. For consider your calling, brothers, that there are
1:26 not many wise according to flesh, not many powerful, not many wellborn.
Matt. But Jesus said, Allow the little children and do not
19:14 prevent them from coming to Me, for of such is the
kingdom of the heavens.
Col. The mystery which has been hidden from the ages
1:26-27 and from the generations but now has been manifested to His saints; to whom God willed to make
known what are the riches of the glory of this
mystery among the Gentiles, which is Christ in
you, the hope of glory.

The Father has hidden all the things as the contents of His
economy from the wise and the intelligent—the worldlings. In
1 Corinthians 1:26 Paul said, "For consider your calling, brothers, that there are not many wise according to flesh, not many
powerful, not many wellborn." The universities are full of wise
and intelligent men who are blind concerning God's economy.

The Father has revealed these things to the infants—the
Son's believers (Matt. 19:13-14; 1 Cor. 1:27-28). In Matthew 19,
when people brought the infants to the Lord Jesus, the disciples rebuked them. But the Lord said, "Allow the little children
and do not prevent them from coming to Me, for of such is the
kingdom of the heavens" (v. 14). If we are wise and intelligent
and not as children, there is no hope for us to enter into the
kingdom of the heavens.

It is the Father's pleasant will to hide the contents of His
economy from the wise and intelligent, the worldlings, and
reveal them to infants, the Son's believers. (*The God-man
Living*, pp. 119-120)

Today's Reading

Matthew 11:26 says, "Yes, Father, for thus it has been well-
pleasing in Your sight." It was well-pleasing in the Father's
sight that the Son was rejected. The Father was glad to see the

Son's rejection. It is very difficult for us to believe this. If your parents and relatives would be one with you regarding the Lord's recovery, you would be excited and praise the Lord. But you must praise the Lord as you are experiencing rejection, saying, "I praise You, Father, because You are the Lord of the heavens and of the earth. All things are of You, and I praise You for this situation."

Verse 27 says, "All things have been delivered to Me by My Father." "All things" refers to all the remnant whom the Father has given the Son (John 3:27; 6:37, 44, 65; 18:9). This word implies that the wise and intelligent rejected the Son because the Father was not pleased to give them to the Son. However, all the remnant has been delivered to the Son by the Father. Peter, John, James, and Andrew were some of those given to the Son by the Father. The Lord Jesus said, "All that the Father gives Me will come to Me, and him who comes to Me I shall by no means cast out" (John 6:37). It is absolutely of the Father's sovereign mercy that we are in the Lord's recovery today. We need to worship the Father for this. Among the many Christians in the world, we are in the recovery. I have the deep sense within that through the years the Lord's recovery has been in this country, He has been reaping a harvest. He has been gathering a remnant among the Christians. During the years we were in Elden hall in Los Angeles, the Lord was gathering His remnant. Month after month, the Lord brought His remnant from various cities, states, and countries. That was a real gathering of the remnant. All those who were gathered together can testify that we were delivered by the Father. The Lord's recovery is not a common Christian work; it is the gathering of the Lord's remnant to recover God's kingdom in the church life. The Lord is still doing the work of gathering His remnant today. (*Life-study of Matthew*, pp. 389-390)

Further Reading: The God-man Living, msgs. 12-13; *Life-study of Matthew,* msg. 31

Enlightenment and inspiration: _____

_____

_____

_____

Morning Nourishment

Matt. All things have been delivered to Me by My
11:27 Father, and no one fully knows the Son except
the Father; neither does anyone fully know the
Father except the Son and him to whom the Son
wills to reveal *Him*.

16:16- And Simon Peter answered and said, You are the
17 Christ, the Son of the living God. And Jesus
answered and said to him, Blessed are you,
Simon Barjona, because flesh and blood has not
revealed *this* to you, but My Father who is in the
heavens.

Phil. To know Him and the power of His resurrection
3:10 and the fellowship of His sufferings, being conformed to His death.

The Lord's prayer is surpassing, and His teaching is unveiling (Matt. 11:27-30). As the infants, we are unveiled, because
the Lord has taken away all the veils from us.

No one fully knows the Son except the Father; neither does
anyone fully know the Father except the Son and him to whom
the Son wills to reveal Him (Matt. 11:27). Concerning the Son,
only the Father has such knowledge, and concerning the Father, only the Son and he to whom the Son reveals Him have
such knowledge. Hence, to know the Son requires that the
Father reveal Him (16:17), and to know the Father requires
that the Son reveal Him (John 17:6, 26). Paul aspired in
Philippians 3:10 to know Christ. To know Christ is the preeminent thing. Christ is all-inclusive, all-extensive, and unlimited.
(*The God-man Living,* pp. 112-113)

Today's Reading

The Lord's surpassing prayer and His unveiling teaching
in Matthew 11:25-30 are regarding four major items: regarding God's eternal economy, regarding God's pleasant will, regarding the first God-man as the Head of the Body, the

prototype, and the model, and regarding His believers as the members of His Body, His mass production, and His duplication. The mass production is from the prototype, and the duplication is from the model.

God's eternal economy is seen in Matthew 11:27, where the Lord says, "All things have been delivered to Me by My Father, and no one fully knows the Son except the Father; neither does anyone fully know the Father except the Son and him to whom the Son wills to reveal Him."

The Father has delivered all His elect to the Son for the building up of the Son's Body (v. 27a; John 6:37, 44, 65; 17:6b; 18:9). God the Father has given all His chosen ones to the Son, not for them to go to heaven or merely for their salvation but for the building up of the Body of Christ. The Son needs a Body and the Triune God needs an organism. The Body of Christ is the Triune God's organism for His expression and enlargement. Physically speaking, our body is our enlargement. The Body of Christ as the organism is the enlargement of Christ as the Head. All the elect given to the Son by the Father are the enlargement of Christ and the organism of the Triune God to express Him.

Only the Father knows the Son as the centrality and universality of His economy (Matt. 11:27b; cf. Col. 2:2; Matt. 16:15-17; Gal. 1:15-16; Eph. 3:4; Phil. 3:10). Christ the Son is the mystery of God. God has His person and His purpose. God's person is triune. His Trinity is His person. The content of the New Testament is the Triune God. Every chapter of Ephesians reveals the Triune God (see note 1 of 2 Corinthians 13:14—Recovery Version). Chapter one reveals that God has blessed us in a threefold way. In the Father, He has chosen us; in the Son, He has redeemed us; and in the Spirit, He seals us and is our guarantee. The economy of the Triune God is for Him to dispense Himself into His chosen and redeemed people to make them His expression. (*The God-man Living,* pp. 117-118)

Further Reading: The God-man Living, msgs. 12-13

Enlightenment and inspiration: _____

_____

_____

_____

Morning Nourishment

Col. And He is before all things, and all things cohere in
1:17-18 Him; and He is the Head of the Body, the church; He
is the beginning, the Firstborn from the dead, that
He Himself might have the first place in all things.
Rev. John to the seven churches which are in Asia:
1:4 Grace to you and peace from Him who is and who
was and who is coming, and from the seven Spirits
who are before His throne.
John I have manifested Your name to the men whom You
17:6 gave Me out of the world. They were Yours, and You
gave them to Me, and they have kept Your word.

The Triune God's economy was made according to His
purpose for His good pleasure, and His good pleasure comes
out of His heart's desire. God is a living person, full of feeling.
He has His heart's desire. Out of God's heart's desire is God's
good pleasure. Out of this pleasure is God's purpose, and out
of this purpose is His economy. The entire Bible is the contents
of God's economy.

Christ as God came to be a man for God's economy. He is
the centrality and universality of God. In January 1934
Brother Watchman Nee gave a conference on Christ being the
centrality and universality of God. He is the hub, the rim, and
the spokes—the entire content—of God's economy. The first
conference I gave in the United States was on the all-inclusive
Christ typified by the good land from only three verses—
Deuteronomy 8:7-9. To know Christ, as Paul said in Philippians 3:10, is not a small thing, because He is everything. To
know any other person is simple because that person is not
all-inclusive. (*The God-man Living*, p. 118)

Today's Reading

Christ was God becoming a man, and this man who was in
the flesh, as the last Adam, became a life-giving Spirit (1 Cor.
15:45b). This life-giving Spirit is compounded with the Divine
Trinity, divinity, humanity, Christ's death with its effectiveness,

and His resurrection with its power. All these items are compounded into the compound Spirit typified by the anointing ointment in Exodus 30. Also, this compounded, life-giving Spirit became intensified sevenfold (Rev. 1:4; 4:5; 5:6). The New Testament reveals Christ in the flesh in the Gospels, Christ as the life-giving Spirit in the Epistles, and Christ as the sevenfold intensified life-giving Spirit in Revelation. No one can know Christ the Son in an exhaustive way except the Father. The Son is the Father's word, explanation, definition, and expression.

Only the Son knows the Father as the source and Maker of His economy (Matt. 11:27c). No one fully knows the Father except the Son and those believers to whom the Son wills to reveal the Father. The four Gospels show us God the Father. No other book reveals the Father as much as the Gospel of John does. We have seen that the Lord Jesus extolled the Father as the Lord of heaven and earth (v. 25). He praised the Father with acknowledgment.

The Son reveals the Father to His believers for the formation of His Body (v. 27d; John 17:6a). God's economy is for the expression of the Father through the Son with His organism, the Body of Christ. The New Testament teaches that the Father as the source has a desire to have an organism through the Son, and the Son came to call God's elect to come to Him so that He can regenerate, sanctify, and transform them, making them His Body to be the organism of the Triune God.

The New Testament teaches us, the members of the Body of Christ, to do everything with God, in God, by God, and through God. It does not teach us to love people in an ethical way with our natural love. We have to love others by and with God, in a divine and mystical way. His love is divine, but the outward lover is a mystical human. The Bible teaches us to live as divine and mystical persons. (*The God-man Living,* pp. 118-119)

Further Reading: The God-man Living, msgs. 12-13

Enlightenment and inspiration: _____

_____

_____

_____

Morning Nourishment

Matt.   Come to Me all who toil and are burdened, and I
11:28-29   will give you rest. Take My yoke upon you and
learn from Me, for I am meek and lowly in heart,
and you will find rest for your souls.

John   Truly, truly, I say to you, Unless the grain of wheat
12:24   falls into the ground and dies, it abides alone; but
if it dies, it bears much fruit.

Matt.   And going forward a little, He fell on His face and
26:39   prayed, saying, My Father, if it is possible, let this
cup pass from Me; yet not as I will, but as You *will.*

The first God-man is the Head of the Body, the prototype,
and the model (Matt. 11:29a). He came as one grain of wheat
to produce many grains (John 12:24). The one grain was the
prototype, and the many grains are the mass production. The
mass production is the duplication of the model. Peter told us
that Christ is a model to the believers (1 Pet. 2:21). The Greek
word for *model* is literally a writing copy, an underwriting used
by students to trace letters and thereby learn to draw them.
We become the reproduction of Christ as the original writing
copy. Christ is the prototype to produce a mass production and
the model to produce the many duplications.

Christ was the first God-man, and we are the many God-
men. We have to learn of Him in His absolute submission to
God and His uttermost satisfaction with God. Christ was so
submissive to and satisfied with the Father and His will. (*The
God-man Living,* p. 120)

Today's Reading

In Matthew 11:28 the Lord sounded out a call: "Come to Me
all who toil and are burdened, and I will give you rest." The
Lord seemed to be saying, "All you who labor and are burdened,
come to Me and rest. All you religious people and all you
worldly people who are laboring and are burdened, come to Me
and I will give you rest." What a gracious word! The toil
mentioned in verse 28 refers not only to the labor of striving

to keep the commandments of the law and religious regulations, but also to the labor of struggling to be successful in any work. Whoever labors thus is always heavily burdened. After the Lord had praised the Father, acknowledging the Father's way and declaring the divine economy, He called this kind of people to come to Him for rest. Rest refers not only to being set free from labor and burden under the law and religion or under any work and responsibility, but also to perfect peace and full satisfaction.

In verse 29 the Lord tells us to learn from Him. He is meek and lowly in heart. To be meek means not to resist any opposition, and to be lowly means not to esteem oneself highly. In all the opposition the Lord was meek, and in all the rejection He was lowly in heart. He submitted Himself fully to the will of His Father, not wanting to do anything for Himself nor expecting to gain something for Himself. Hence, regardless of the situation, He had rest in His heart. He was fully satisfied with His Father's will.

The Lord said that if we take His yoke upon us and learn from Him, we shall find rest to our souls. The rest we find by taking the Lord's yoke and learning from Him is for our souls. It is an inward rest; it is not anything merely outward in nature.

If we are opposed as we minister, and we resist, we shall not have peace. But if instead of resisting we submit to the will of the Father, testifying that the opposition is of the Father, we shall have rest in our souls. John the Baptist did not regard his imprisonment as of the Father; therefore, he was not at rest. If he had realized that his imprisonment was due to the Father's will, he would have been at rest, even in prison. Christ, the heavenly King, always submitted to the Father's will, taking God's will as His portion and not resisting anything. Hence, He was always at rest. We must learn of Him and also take this view. If we do, we shall have rest in our souls. (*Life-study of Matthew,* pp. 390-392)

Further Reading: The God-man Living, msgs. 12-13; *Life-study of Matthew,* msg. 31

Enlightenment and inspiration: _____

_____
_____

Morning Nourishment

Matt. 11:29-30 Take My yoke upon you and learn from Me, for I am meek and lowly in heart, and you will find rest for your souls. For My yoke is easy and My burden is light.

1 Pet. 2:21 For to this you were called, because Christ also suffered on your behalf, leaving you a model so that you may follow in His steps.

Rom. 12:1 I exhort you therefore, brothers, through the compassions of God to present your bodies a living sacrifice, holy, well pleasing to God, *which* is your reasonable service.

In Matthew 11:29 and 30 we have the way to rest: "Take My yoke upon you and learn from Me, for I am meek and lowly in heart, and you will find rest for your souls. For My yoke is pleasant and My burden is light." The Lord's yoke is to take the will of the Father. It is not to be regulated or controlled by any obligations of the law or religion, nor to be enslaved by any work, but to be constrained by the will of the Father. The Lord lived such a life, caring for nothing but the will of His Father (John 4:34; 5:30; 6:38). He submitted Himself fully to the Father's will (26:39, 42). Hence, He asks us to learn from Him. God's will is our yoke. Thus, we are not free to do as we please; rather, we are yoked. Young people, do not think that you are so free or liberated. In the Lord's recovery we all have been yoked. How good it is to be yoked! The Lord's yoke is easy and His burden is light. The Lord's yoke is the Father's will, and His burden is the work to carry out the Father's will. Such a yoke is easy, not bitter, and such a burden is light, not heavy. The Greek word rendered *pleasant* signifies fit for use; hence, good, kindly, mild, gentle, easy, pleasant, in contrast to what is hard, harsh, sharp, and bitter. (*Life-study of Matthew,* pp. 391-392)

Today's Reading

The Lord assured the disciples that His yoke is easy and His burden is light (Matt. 11:30). The Greek word for *easy* means "fit for use"; hence, good, kind, mild, gentle, easy, pleasant—in contrast to hard, harsh, sharp, bitter. The yoke of God's economy is like this. Everything in God's economy is not a heavy burden but an enjoyment.

The Lord's believers answer His call in their heart and come to Him bodily (Matt. 11:28a). To come to Him bodily means that our entire being has to come to Him. This is why Paul charges us in Romans 12:1 to present our bodies to the Lord as a living sacrifice. We have to present our bodies in a practical way by being in the meetings of the church. Since I was saved by the Lord in 1925, I have come to Him with my entire being.

The believers copy the Lord in their spirit by taking His yoke—God's will—and toiling for God's economy according to His model (Matt. 11:29a; 1 Pet. 2:21). The Lord told us to learn from Him. To learn from Him is to copy Him, not to imitate Him outwardly. In this way we become His duplication and mass production. The first requirement in learning from Him is to take His yoke, which is God's will. God's will has to yoke us, and we have to put our neck into this yoke. Seventy years ago as a young man, I took the yoke of Jesus. That yoke has protected me for the past seventy years.

We also need to be those who toil for God's economy. All the worldly people are toiling and are burdened in many things. They are very busy. The Lord is calling those who are toiling, who are burdened, and who have no rest or satisfaction, to come to Him so that He can give them the real rest with satisfaction. The rest without satisfaction is not the real rest. We take His yoke and toil for God's economy according to His model, following Him in His footsteps.

The hardest thing is to rest in our soul. People lose sleep because their soul is bothered. The rest that we find by taking the Lord's yoke and learning from Him is for our soul. We share in our soul His rest in satisfaction (Matt. 11:28b, 29b, 30). (*The God-man Living,* pp. 113-114, 121-122)

Further Reading: Life-study of Matthew, msg. 31; *The God-man Living,* msgs. 12-13

Enlightenment and inspiration: _____

_____

Hymns, #403

1   Live Thyself, Lord Jesus, through me,
         For my very life art Thou;
     Thee I take to all my problems
         As the full solution now.
     Live Thyself, Lord Jesus, through me,
         In all things Thy will be done;
     I but a transparent vessel
         To make visible the Son.

2   Consecrated is Thy temple,
         Purged from every stain and sin;
     May Thy flame of glory now be
         Manifested from within.
     Let the earth in solem wonder
         See my body willingly
     Offered as Thy slave obedient,
         Energized alone by Thee.

3   Every moment, every member,
         Girded, waiting Thy command;
     Underneath the yoke to labor
         Or be laid aside as planned.
     When restricted in pursuing,
         No disquiet will beset;
     Underneath Thy faithful dealing
         Not a murmur or regret.

4   Ever tender, quiet, restful,
         Inclinations put away,
     That Thou may for me choose freely
         As Thy finger points the way.
     Live Thyself, Lord Jesus, through me,
         For my very life art Thou;
     Thee I take to all my problems
         As the full solution now.

Composition for prophecy with main point and sub-points: _____

_____

_____

_____

_____

_____

_____

_____

_____

_____

_____

_____

_____

_____

_____

_____

_____

_____

_____

_____

_____

_____

_____

_____

_____

_____

_____

_____

_____

_____

_____

_____

_____

_____

_____

_____

_____

_____

_____

_____

_____

The Lord's Training His Disciples
to Learn from Him as a Man of Prayer

Scripture Reading: Matt. 14:19, 22-23; 6:6

Day 1   I. In the performing of the miracle of feeding five thousand people with five loaves and two fish, the Lord trained His disciples to learn from Him (Matt. 11:29):

A. To see the miracle of feeding five thousand with five loaves and two fish is easy, but to know the deeper and greater lessons of life, which we have to learn from the Performer of this great miracle, requires revelation (cf. v. 25).

B. These lessons are intrinsic, deeper, and of life; we need to learn these living lessons from the Lord so that we can enter into the God-man living.

C. Matthew 14:19 says that He took the five loaves and two fish, and when He was going to bless them, He looked up to heaven:

1. *Looking up to heaven* indicates that He was looking up to His source, His Father in heaven:

a. This indicates that He realized the source of the blessing was not Him; the Father as the sending One, not the sent One, should be the source of blessing (cf. Rom. 11:36).

b. Regardless of how much we can do or how much we know what to do, we must realize that we need the Sender's blessing upon our doing so that we can be channels of supply by trusting in Him, not in ourselves (cf. Matt. 14:19b; Num. 6:22-27).

Day 2   2. His looking up to the Father in heaven indicated that as the Son on earth sent by the Father in heaven, He was one with the Father, trusting in the Father (John 10:30):

a. What I know and what I can do mean nothing; being one with the Lord and

trusting in Him mean everything in our
ministry (cf. 1 Cor. 2:3-4).

b. The blessing comes only by our being
one with the Lord and trusting in Him
(cf. 2 Cor. 1:8-9).

3. The Lord did not do anything from Himself
(John 5:19; cf. Matt. 16:24):

a. We should deny ourselves and not have
the intention of doing anything from ourselves but have the intention of doing
everything from Him.

b. We need to continually exercise our spirit
to reject the self and live by another life
by the bountiful supply of the Spirit of
Jesus Christ (Phil. 1:19-21a).

Day 3

4. The Lord did not seek His own will but the
will of Him who sent Him (John 5:30b; 6:38;
Matt. 26:39, 42):

a. He rejected His idea, His intention, and
His purpose.

b. All of us should be on the alert for this one
thing—when we are sent to do some work,
we should not take that chance to seek our
own goal; we should just go, seeking the
idea, purpose, aim, goal, and intention of
our sending Lord (cf. 1 Tim. 5:2b).

5. The Lord did not seek His own glory, but the
glory of the Father who sent Him (John 7:18;
5:41; cf. 12:43):

a. To be ambitious is to seek your own glory
(cf. 3 John 9).

b. We need to see that our self, our purpose,
and our ambition are three big destroying
"worms" in our work; we must learn to
hate them.

c. If we are going to be used for the Lord always
in His recovery, our self has to be denied, our
purpose has to be rejected, and our ambition must be given up (Matt. 16:24).

Day 4
II. **After performing the miracle, the Lord went up to the mountain privately to pray (Matt. 14:23; cf. Luke 6:12):**

A. The Lord did not remain in the issue of the miracle with the crowds but went away from them privately to be with the Father on the mountain in prayer:

1. The word *privately* is very meaningful; this means He did not let people know He was going to pray:

a. The Lord compelled the disciples to leave Him in order that He might have more time to pray privately to the Father (Matt. 14:22-23).

b. He needed to pray privately to His Father who was in the heavens, that He might be one with the Father and have the Father with Him in whatever He did on earth for the establishing of the kingdom of the heavens.

Day 5
2. The Lord told us, "When you pray, enter into your private room, and shut your door and pray to your Father who is in secret; and your Father who sees in secret will repay you" (6:6):

a. When we pray with others, we cannot enjoy the Lord as deeply as when we pray to the Lord privately.

b. The kingdom people must have some experience of prayer in their private room, contacting their heavenly Father in secret, experiencing some secret enjoyment of the Father, and receiving some secret answer from Him:

(1) The self is most visible in the fact that it enjoys doing things in a public way, in the presence of man; the self loves to be glorified, and the flesh loves to be gazed upon.

(2) If you pray every day without telling
    others or letting them know about it,
    it means that you are healthy and
    that you are growing.

(3) If you always tell others how much
    you pray, you will not only lose your
    reward but also not grow in life or be
    healthy (cf. 13:6).

Day 6

3. We have to learn to leave the crowds, our
   family, our friends, and the saints in the
   church to go to a higher level on a "high
   mountain," separated from the crowd, to be
   with the Father privately and secretly to
   have intimate fellowship with Him (cf. Exo.
   33:11a).

B. His going up to the mountain privately to pray
   indicated His asking the Father to bless all
   those who had participated in the enjoyment
   of the issue of the miracle that they would not
   be satisfied with the food which perishes, but
   that they should seek for the food which abides
   unto eternal life (John 6:27).

C. His going up to the mountain privately to pray
   also indicated that He wanted to receive from
   the Father some instruction concerning how to
   take care of the five thousand people fed by
   His miracle.

Morning Nourishment

Matt. Take My yoke upon you and learn from Me, for I
11:29 am meek and lowly in heart, and you will find
rest for your souls.

14:19 And after commanding the crowds to recline on
the grass, He took the five loaves and the two fish,
and looking up to heaven, He blessed and broke
the loaves and gave *them* to the disciples, and the
disciples to the crowds.

There are three very important considerations in God's work
which we should never forget. First, the initiation of God's work
must be according to His will. Second, the advance of God's work
must be according to His power, not our own power. Third, the result
of God's work must be for His glory. If we fail in any of these three
points, we have committed an iniquity against the sanctuary. No
work can be initiated by ourselves, no work can be carried out
by our own strength, and no work should result in our own glory.

In the meetings the sisters have their heads covered with
respect to the brothers. This signifies that everyone is covered
before Christ. He is the Lord, and only He is the Head. Only He
is worthy to be the Lord of all, and only He is worthy to initiate
any work. In God's work, no decision should be made through the
discussion of two or three brothers. The result and worth of a
work, whether or not it is spiritual and pleasing to God, depend
not on the amount of work that has been done, but on how much
of the work is initiated by ourselves and how much is initiated
by God. The less we initiate, the more spiritual, worthwhile, and
acceptable it is to God. I thank God that I do not have to initiate
anything. He arranges everything. I do not have to be respon-
sible for coming up with anything. We often think that we
should do this or that, but God has His own agenda. We do not
have to be His counselor. We only need to do His will and find
out if something is according to His will. We do not have to worry
about the result. The initiation of God's work must be His will
and His will alone. We have no right to initiate anything. God's
will must be the unique beginning of all His works. (Watchman
Nee, *The Collected Works of Watchman Nee*, vol. 42, pp. 359-360)

Today's Reading

In the performing of the miracle of feeding five thousand people with five loaves and two fish, He trained His disciples to learn from Him. In Matthew 11:29 the Lord told the disciples that they needed to learn from Him, indicating that He was their pattern.

[In Matthew 14:19 the Lord] blessed the food by looking up to heaven. *Looking up to heaven* indicates that He was looking up to His Father in heaven. This indicates that He realized the source of the blessing was not Him. He was the sent One. The sent One should not be the source of blessing. The sending One, the Father, should be the source of blessing.

Here is a great lesson for us to learn....We need to see the pattern which the Lord set up for us here. We need to remember that He looked up to the Father in heaven and blessed the five loaves and two fish in front of His disciples. After His blessing in this way, He told the disciples what to do. No doubt, what He did was a pattern for the disciples to learn from Him. According to this pattern, we have to realize that we are not the Sender, but the ones sent by the Sender. Regardless of how much we can do, we should realize that we still need the blessing from the source, from our Sender, that we can pass on to the benefited ones. This is a big lesson which I want to stress.

A co-worker who is invited to speak somewhere may think that since he has been speaking for the Lord for many years, he knows how to speak. All of us need to drop this kind of attitude and realize that we are not the source. No blessing is of us. Regardless of how much we can do or how much we know what to do, we must realize that we need the Sender's blessing upon our doing by trusting in Him, not in ourselves. Even when we take our meals, we should learn of the Lord to look up to the Father as the source. When we bless our food, we should bless it by looking up to the source of blessing. (*The God-man Living*, pp. 125-126)

Further Reading: The Collected Works of Watchman Nee, vol. 42, ch. 45; *The God-man Living,* msg. 14

Enlightenment and inspiration: _____

Morning Nourishment

John Then Jesus answered and said to them, Truly,
5:19 truly, I say to you, The Son can do nothing from
Himself except what He sees the Father doing, for
whatever that One does, these things the Son also
does in like manner.
10:30 I and the Father are one.
1 Cor. And I was with you in weakness and in fear and
2:3-4 in much trembling; and my speech and my proclamation were not in persuasive words of wisdom
but in demonstration of the Spirit and of power.

[The Lord's] looking up to the Father in heaven [Matt.
14:19] indicated that as the Son on earth sent by the Father in
heaven, He was one with the Father, trusting in the Father
(John 10:30). This is a very important principle. Whenever I
speak for the Lord, I must have the sensation that I am one
with the Lord, trusting in Him. What I know and what I can
do mean nothing. Being one with the Lord and trusting in Him
mean everything in our ministry. We should never go to minister the word by remaining in ourselves and by trusting in
what we can do. If we trust in what we can do, we are finished.
The blessing comes only by our being one with the Lord and
trusting in Him. (*The God-man Living*, p. 126)

Today's Reading

[Jesus] is God becoming a man, a real man. Yet this Man would
not live by Himself, by His own human life. Rather, He rejected
His human life. He denied Himself. He lived as a man by another
life, by the life of God. He told us that whatever He did and
whatever He spoke were not of Himself but of the Father who
sent Him (John 14:10, 24). He was a real man living there, yet
He was dying to His natural life. He was dying to live, dying to
His natural man to live by God's life. That dying to His natural
life is the cross, and His living by the divine life is in resurrection.

For thirty-three and a half years, this God-man, Jesus, was
a genuine man, but He lived not by man's life but by God's life.

To live such a life He had to be crucified. The crucifixion mentioned in the New Testament transpired on the wooden cross on Mount Calvary. But you have to realize that before Christ was there in the physical crucifixion, He was being crucified every day for thirty-three and a half years. Was not Jesus a human being, a genuine man? Yes. But He did not live by that genuine man. Instead, He kept that genuine man on the cross. Then, in the sense of resurrection, He lived God's life. God's life with all its attributes was lived within this God-man Jesus and expressed as this God-man's virtues.

After my thirty-two years of ministry in the United States, I have the assurance that a number of you have been perfected. What is it to be perfected? It is to be matured by continually exercising to reject the self and live by another life. This is according to what Paul said: "I am crucified with Christ; and it is no longer I who live, but it is Christ who lives in me" (Gal. 2:20a). Paul lived by dying to live. He was dying to his natural man and living by his new man with the divine life. So he said that by the bountiful supply of the Spirit of Jesus Christ, he lived and magnified Christ (Phil. 1:19-21a).

We should not live by ourselves. According to God's design in His economy we were already put on the cross. We should not call ourselves back off the cross. To remain on the cross is to bear the cross and be under the cross. I have been crucified. There is no more I. I am finished. I am through. But there is a new man with me. That is the resurrected God-created man uplifted with God's divinity in him. That man is actually God Himself. Now I live by that man. But if I do not practice to keep my old man on the cross, I can never live the new man. This is why in the first chapter of Philippians, Paul told us he lived such a life by the bountiful supply of the Spirit of Jesus Christ. (*The Practical Points concerning Blending,* pp. 34-36)

Further Reading: The God-man Living, msg. 14; *The Practical Points concerning Blending,* ch. 4*

Enlightenment and inspiration: _____
_____
_____
_____

Morning Nourishment

John **I can do nothing from Myself; as I hear, I judge,**
5:30 **and My judgment is just, because I do not seek My own will but the will of Him who sent Me.**

6:38 **For I have come down from heaven not to do My own will but the will of Him who sent Me.**

7:18 **He who speaks from himself seeks his own glory; but He who seeks the glory of Him who sent Him, this One is true, and unrighteousness is not in Him.**

The Lord did not seek His own will but the will of Him who sent Him (John 5:30b). First, He denied Himself; second, He rejected His idea, His intention, and His purpose. He would only seek the will of the One who sent Him. All of us should be on the alert for this one thing—when we are sent to do some work, we should not take that chance to seek our own goal. When we go to perform God's work, do we go by seeking our purpose or God's purpose? Brother Watchman Nee was always concerned that when he sent a brother out for the Lord's work, that brother would take the chance to perform his own purpose.

One day I was preparing to go from Shanghai to Hangchow. Then Brother Nee asked me, "Witness, for what purpose are you going to Hangchow?" I responded that I was going to visit the brothers there. He said that this was a wrong answer. Instead, I should say that I am going to perform the Lord's purpose. If you merely go to visit the brothers, you can do many things for yourself. You may take your visit to them as a chance for you to accomplish your purpose instead of seeking the Lord's will. It is not easy to have a pure heart, without having our purpose, our goal, and our idea. We should just go seeking the idea, purpose, goal, and intention of the sending Lord. This requires much learning on our part. (*The God-man Living*, p. 127)

Today's Reading

At times certain brothers may ask me how I feel about their accepting the invitation to a certain place. My basic consideration is, "Are you going just to fulfill the Lord's purpose, the Lord's aim, the Lord's goal, the Lord's idea, the Lord's intention, that is, the Lord's will, or would you take the chance to accomplish your intention, your will?" To seek our intention is absolutely impure. We need to be purified by the cross. We should pray, "Lord, save me from going out to accomplish something according to my intention and idea." The Lord Jesus never sought His own idea, His own purpose, His own concept, or His own intention. He purely sought only the Father's will.

The first God-man did not seek His own glory but the glory of the Father who sent Him (John 7:18). I was with Brother Nee for about twenty years. What bothered him the most about the co-workers was that it was hard to see one who was not ambitious. To be ambitious is to seek your own glory. In the service we render to the Lord in the church life, there is always our ambition....We are all fallen descendants of Adam and sick of the same disease, the same sin....Through the years I have seen a number of co-workers among us spoiled by ambition. By the Lord's mercy, I have learned the secret of dealing with my self and my intention, and this has helped me to deal with my self-glorification.

In John 7:18 the Lord [was speaking to the Pharisees.]...The Pharisees were seeking their own glory. According to the context of this verse, the Lord indicated to them that if they were not seeking their own glory, they would know that He was sent by His Father.

We need to see that our self, our purpose, and our ambition are three big destroying "worms" in our work. If we are going to be used for the Lord always in His recovery, our self has to be denied, our purpose has to be rejected, and our ambition must be given up. We should not have our own purpose; instead, we should have only the Lord's will. We all have to learn of these three things: no self, no purpose, and no ambition. We should only know to labor, to work for Him, by denying our self, rejecting our purpose, and giving up our ambition. (*The God-man Living,* pp. 127-128)

Further Reading: The God-man Living, msg. 14; *Life-study of 1 Timothy,* msg. 9

Enlightenment and inspiration: _____

_____

Morning Nourishment

Matt. And immediately He compelled the disciples to step
14:22-23 into the boat and to go before Him to the other side,
while He sent the crowds away. And after He sent the
crowds away, He went up to the mountain privately
to pray. And when night fell, He was there alone.
Luke And in these days He went out to the mountain to
6:12 pray, and He spent the whole night in prayer to God.

After performing the miracle, the Lord went up to the
mountain privately to pray (Matt. 14:23; cf. Luke 6:12).

The Lord did not remain in the issue of the miracle with the
crowds but went away from them privately to be with the
Father on the mountain in prayer. If we go to a certain place
and have a great success, would we leave right away or would
we remain in this big success to enjoy it? We need to see and
follow the pattern of the Lord Jesus. He did not remain in the
issue of the great miracle which He performed. Instead, He
went up to the mountain privately to pray. The word *privately*
is very meaningful. This means He did not let the people know
He was going to pray. Otherwise, they would have followed Him.
He went away from them privately to be with the Father in
prayer. I like these three phrases: *to be with the Father, on the
mountain,* and *in prayer.* We should learn from the Lord's
pattern here by exercising to be with Him on the mountain in
prayer. His looking up to heaven means that He had no trust
in Himself. His going up to the mountain means that He wanted
to be with the Father in prayer. (*The God-man Living,* p. 129)

Today's Reading

[Matthew 14:23 indicates that] the heavenly King, as the
beloved Son of the Father (3:17), standing in the position of man
(4:4), needed to pray privately to His Father who is in heaven,
that He might be one with the Father and have the Father with
Him in whatever He did on earth for the establishment of the
kingdom of the heavens. He did this not in the desert, but on
the mountain, leaving all the people, even His disciples, that He

might contact the Father alone.

Our Father sees in secret. As you are praying alone in your room, no one else can see you, but your heavenly Father sees. Do not pray on the street corner or in the synagogues to be seen by men. Pray in secret to be seen by your Father who sees in secret. Then you will also receive an answer from Him in secret. I am concerned that many of us have experiences only in the open and that we do not have any experiences in secret. Not only does the Father see our experiences; everyone else sees them as well. This indicates that we are not rejecting the self or repudiating the flesh. We must always do things in such a way as to constantly reject the self and repudiate the flesh. If possible, do everything in secret, not giving any opportunity to your self or yielding any ground to your flesh.

Although the Lord speaks about the matter of reward (Matt. in life. The saints who grow openly do not grow in a healthy way. We all need some secret growth in life, some secret experiences of Christ. We need to pray to the Lord, worship the Lord, contact the Lord, and fellowship with the Lord in a secret way. Perhaps not even the one closest to us will know or understand what we are doing. We need these secret experiences of the Lord because such experiences kill our self and our flesh. Although anger and lust are ugly, the thing that most frustrates us from growing in life is the self. The self is most visible in the fact that it enjoys doing things in a public way, in the presence of man. The self likes to do righteous deeds before man. We all must admit that, without exception, we have such a self. Those who always want to do things in such a way as to make a public show are full of self, full of the flesh. The self loves to be glorified, and the flesh loves to be gazed upon. Probably you have never heard a message on these verses that dealt with the self and the flesh. Whenever we come to this portion of the Word, we must realize that it exposes our self and our flesh. (*Life-study of Matthew,* pp. 522, 260)

Further Reading: The God-man Living, msg. 14; *Life-study of Matthew,* msgs. 21, 44

Enlightenment and inspiration: _____

_____

Morning Nourishment

Matt. And when you pray, you shall not be like the
6:5-6 hypocrites, because they love to pray standing in
the synagogues and on the street corners, so that
they may be seen by men. Truly I say to you, They
have their reward in full. But you, when you pray,
enter into your private room, and shut your door
and pray to your Father who is in secret; and your
Father who sees in secret will repay you.
13:6 But when the sun rose, they were scorched; and
because they had no root, they withered.

In praying, as in giving alms, the kingdom people are not to
make a public show [Matt. 6:5]....Prayer to seek man's praise
may gain a reward from men, but it does not receive an answer
from the Father. Thus, it is vain prayer.

Our prayer should be in secret [v. 6]....The kingdom people
must have some experience of prayer in their private room,
contacting their heavenly Father in secret, experiencing some
secret enjoyment of the Father, and receiving some secret
answer from Him. (*Life-study of Matthew*, pp. 264-265)

Today's Reading

To repeat, the crucial matter [in Matthew 6:5-6] is not the
reward, but the growth in life. Those saints who know only to
make a show of the self and a display of the flesh will not grow
in life. The genuine growth in life is to cut off the self. Those
whose self has been cut off and whose flesh has been dealt with
may sometimes speak concerning their deeds. However, I am
quite cautious in saying even this. It is not healthy to expose
our righteous deeds. Rather, we should pray much, yet not let
others know how much we pray. This is healthy. If you pray
every day without telling others or letting them know about it,
it means that you are healthy and that you are growing.
However, suppose you always tell others how much you pray. If
you do this, you will not only lose your reward, but you will not

grow in life or be healthy. We all must admit that we have the subtle self, the subtle flesh, within us. We all have such a weak point. When we pray alone in our room, we often wish that others could hear us. Likewise, we do our righteous deeds with the intention that others could see them. Such desires and intentions are not healthy; they indicate that we are not growing in life. Making a public display before men will never help us grow in life. If you want to grow and be healthy in the spiritual life, you must slay the self in the doing of righteous deeds. No matter what kind of righteous deeds we do—giving material things to the saints, praying, fasting, doing something to please God—we must try our best to do them in secret. If your righteous deeds are in secret, you may be assured that you are growing in life and are healthy. But any time you exhibit yourself in your righteous deeds, you are not healthy. Such an exhibition greatly frustrates your growth in life.

The universe indicates that God is hidden, that God is secret. Although He has done a great many things, people are not aware that He has done them. We may have seen the things done by God, but none of us has ever seen Him, for He is always hidden, always secret. God's life is of such a secret and hidden nature. If we love others by our own life, this life will seek to make a display of itself before men. But if we love others by the love of God, this love will always remain hidden. Our human life loves to make a display, a public show, but God's life is always hidden....Although God has so much within Him, only a little is manifested. If we live by this divine life, we may pray much, but others will not know how much we have prayed. We may give a great deal to help others, but no one will know how much we give. We may fast often, but this also will not be known by others. We may have a great deal within us, but very little will be manifested. This is the nature of the kingdom people in the doing of their righteous deeds. (*Life-study of Matthew,* pp. 260-262)

Further Reading: Life-study of Matthew, msg. 21; *The God-man Living,* msg. 14

Enlightenment and inspiration: _____

_____

_____

_____

Morning Nourishment

Exo.   And Jehovah would speak to Moses face to face,
33:11 just as a man speaks to his companion....
John   Work not for the food which perishes, but for the
6:27   food which abides unto eternal life, which the
       Son of Man will give you; for Him has the Father,
       even God, sealed.

To pray with others is good, but often we need to pray by
ourselves. When we pray with others, we cannot enjoy the Lord
as deeply as when we pray to the Lord privately. Even the Lord
Jesus told us that when we pray we should shut our door
privately and pray secretly to the Father who sees in secret
(Matt. 6:6). Then we have the sensation of how intimate He is
to us and how close we are to Him. We have to learn to leave
the crowds, our family, our friends, and the saints in the church
to go to a higher level on a "high mountain." We have to go
higher, far away from the earthly things on a lower level. We
need to get to a higher level, separated from the crowd, to be
with the Father privately and secretly to have intimate fellowship with Him. This is the significance of being *on the mountain
in prayer.* (*The God-man Living,* p. 129)

Today's Reading

We need to consider why the Lord Jesus went to the mountain right after this miracle. John 6:27 gives us the reason....
The Lord told the ones whom He fed not to seek the food that
perishes, but to seek the food that abides unto eternal life. I
believe the Lord Jesus went to the mountain to pray in this way:
"Father, I pray to You under Your blessing. Through Your
blessing You fed the five thousand, but Father, they are just
seeking for the food that perishes. I do look unto You that You
would bless them that they would seek the food that abides unto
eternal life. Father, You know that I am Your sent One. Only I
can give them the food that abides unto eternal life, but they do
not know Me in this way. They know only that I can perform a

miracle to feed them with physical food. But they do not know that it is only I who can give them food that is of the eternal life." I believe that the Lord prayed to bless them further in this way.

His going up to the mountain privately to pray indicated His asking the Father to bless all those who had participated in the enjoyment of the issue of the miracle that they would not be satisfied with the food which perishes, but that they should seek for the food which abides unto eternal life and recognize that He was not only the Son of Man but also the Son of God who was sent and sealed by the Father and who could give them eternal life. When the five thousand were being fed by Him, they recognized that He was the capable Son of Man, but they did not realize that He was actually the Son of God who was not only sent but also sealed by the Father. He was the One who could give them the very bread that is related to the eternal life. For this reason,…in John 6 the Lord revealed that He is the bread out of heaven, the bread of life.…To know Him in this way requires a revelation, so He prayed for them privately on the mountain.

His going up to the mountain privately to pray also indicated that He wanted to receive from the Father some instruction concerning how to take care of the five thousand people fed by His miracle.…We need revelation from the Lord to see the intrinsic significance of His word. To see the miracle of feeding five thousand with five loaves and two fish is easy, but to know the deeper lessons which we have to learn from the Performer of this big miracle requires revelation. These lessons are intrinsic, deeper, and of life. To know the great miracle the Lord performed does not give us any life. We can only admire the Lord's outward doing. But to see all the detailed points concerning the lessons of life to learn from the Lord in His way of performing the miracle imparts life to us. We need to learn these living lessons from the Lord so that we can enter into the God-man living. (*The God-man Living,* pp. 130-131)

Further Reading: The God-man Living, msg. 14; *Life-study of Matthew,* msg. 21

Enlightenment and inspiration: _____

_____

_____

Hymns, #784

1   Pray to fellowship with Jesus,
     In the spirit seek His face;
    Ask and listen in His presence,
     Waiting in the secret place.

     Pray to fellowship with Jesus,
      In the spirit seek His face;
     Ask and listen in His presence,
      Waiting in the secret place.

2   Pray to fellowship with Jesus,
     Fully opened from within,
    With thy face unveiled, beholding,
    Single, pure, and genuine.

3   Pray to fellowship with Jesus,
     Seeking Him in confidence;
    Learn to touch Him as the Spirit,
     Looking up in reverence.

4   Pray to fellowship with Jesus,
     Speaking nothing in pretense;
    Ask according to the spirit,
     Praying by the inner sense.

5   Pray to fellowship with Jesus,
     List'ning earnestly to Him;
    Be impressed with His intentions,
     Yielding to Him from within.

6   Pray to fellowship with Jesus,
     Bathing in His countenance;
    Saturated with His beauty,
     Radiate His excellence.

Composition for prophecy with main point and sub-points: _____

_____

_____

_____

_____

_____

_____

_____

_____

_____

_____

_____

_____

_____

_____

_____

_____

_____

_____

_____

_____

_____

_____

_____

_____

_____

_____

_____

_____

_____

_____

_____

_____

_____

_____

A Man of Prayer—
a God-man Who Pursues Christ,
Lives Christ, and Magnifies Christ

Scripture Reading: Phil. 3:10; 1:19-21a; 4:12-13; 1:9; 4:6

Day 1 **I. The practical way to live a life according to the high peak of the divine revelation is to be a God-man (Gal. 2:20; Phil. 1:20-21a):**

A. Christ, the first God-man, made Himself a prototype for the mass reproduction of many brothers—the many God-men (Rom. 8:29):

1. Christ, being both God and man and having both the divine life and the human life, lived a life of humanity, not by His human life but by His divine life (John 5:19).

2. Christ died to Himself that He might live to the Father and that He might live out the divine attributes as His human virtues (v. 30; 8:28).

3. Christ, living always under the cross in His life on earth, expressed not Himself but the Father (14:9-10).

Day 2 B. The believers in Christ, as the brothers of Christ, the many God-men, need to live a life which is a copy, a reproduction, of the life of Christ (1 Pet. 2:21):

1. The intrinsic significance of following Jesus is to become a xerox copy of the first God-man; therefore, to follow Jesus is to live the life of a God-man.

2. The many God-men need to live a life of bearing the cross in the steps of Christ (Matt. 16:24; 1 Pet. 2:21).

3. The many God-men should die to themselves and live to God (2 Cor. 5:15; Gal. 2:19).

4. A life of dying to ourselves and living to
God is for Christ, the first God-man, to be
formed in His many brothers, the many
God-men, for the building up of His organic
Body that the eternal economy of God
might be carried out (4:19; Eph. 4:16).

Day 3 II. **The book of Philippians unveils the living of
a God-man who pursues Christ, lives Christ,
and magnifies Christ (3:10; 1:19-21a; 4:12-13):**

A. The first aspect of the living of a Christ- pursuing
God-man is to pursue to know Christ (3:10a).

B. The life of a Christ-pursuing God-man is a life
of pursuing to know the power of Christ's resurrection (v. 10b).

C. A God-man lives daily under the cross;
hence, the life of a Christ-pursuing God-man
is a life of pursuing to die with Christ to be
conformed to His death by the power of His
resurrection (Rom. 6:6; Matt. 16:24; 1 Cor.
15:31; Phil. 3:10).

D. The life of a Christ-pursuing God-man is a life
of living Christ to magnify Him through the
bountiful supply of the Spirit of Jesus Christ
(1:19-21a).

Day 4 E. A Christ-pursuing God-man lives in the em-
powering Christ and by taking Christ as the
secret in everything (4:12-13).

F. A Christ-pursuing God-man overcomes the
negative things in Philippians: rivalry, mur-
murings and reasonings, seeking our own
things, evil workers, confidence in the flesh,
anxiety, and want (1:17; 2:3, 14, 21; 3:2, 4-8;
4:6, 11).

G. If we live the life of a God-man in resurrection,
a genuine revival will be brought forth from
within us; this will be an unprecedented revival, a revival that has never occurred in the
history of the church (Hab. 3:2; Hosea 6:2).

Day 5 III. **To pray without ceasing by calling on the Lord's name is to live Christ (1 Thes. 5:17; Rom. 10:12-13; Phil. 1:21a):**

A. By calling on the name of the Lord, we automatically take Him as our life and spontaneously live Him (Rom. 10:12-13; Col. 3:4).

B. If we pray, breathing in Christ as our life, we will not do things by ourselves, apart from Christ; instead, by praying without ceasing, we will live Christ.

C. "This I pray, that your love may abound yet more and more in full knowledge and all discernment" (Phil. 1:9):

1. The Philippian believers' love needed to abound more and more, not foolishly but in full discernment, not in ignorance but in full knowledge, that they might prove by testing the things which differed.

2. The knowledge and discernment in 1:9 are Christ Himself; when we experience Christ, He becomes our knowledge and discernment.

D. "I know that...this will turn out to salvation through your petition and the bountiful supply of the Spirit of Jesus Christ" (1:19):

1. If we join verses 7 and 19, we will see that "your petition" indicates the supply of the Body.

2. The reason that Paul speaks of the supply of the Body before the bountiful supply of the Spirit is that the Spirit is upon the Body (Psa. 133):

   a. Paul realized that as a member of the Body, he needed the supply of the Body.

   b. If the Body would be exercised to supply him, the bountiful supply of the Spirit would come to him through the Body.

E. "In nothing be anxious, but in everything, by prayer and petition with thanksgiving, let your requests be made known to God" (Phil. 4:6):
1. Prayer involves conversing with the Lord, communicating with Him in fellowship, and worshipping Him.
2. The Greek *pros* in the phrase "to God" denotes motion toward, in the sense of a living union and communion, implying fellowship:
   a. "To God" conveys the thought of motion toward some object which produces a transaction in the sense of a living union.
   b. The meaning of "to God" here is *in the fellowship with God;* we should let our requests be made known to God in such a fellowship, in such a union and communion.
3. If we ask the Lord about everything and talk with Him in everything, we will receive the Lord's element into us, a divine metabolism will work in us, and Christ will be expressed through us; this is to live Christ.
4. We need to practice speaking to the Lord constantly; then spontaneously we will live Christ.

Morning Nourishment

Rom. Because those whom He foreknew, He also pre-
8:29 destinated *to be* conformed to the image of His
Son, that He might be the Firstborn among
many brothers.
John I can do nothing from Myself; as I hear, I judge,
5:30 and My judgment is just, because I do not seek
My own will but the will of Him who sent Me.
14:9 Jesus said to him, Have I been so long a time
with you, and you have not known Me, Philip?
He who has seen Me has seen the Father; how
is it that you say, Show us the Father?

Many Christians know that one day God was incarnated to be a man by the name of Jesus. They know this just in black and white, but sorry to say, they do not know the intrinsic fact of this incarnation. This incarnation produced a God-man, who lived on the earth not by His human life but by His divine life. All the days when He was on earth, He put Himself on the cross. He remained on the cross to die that He might live by God, not to express man but to express God in His divine attributes becoming man's virtues. This was the life of the first God-man as a prototype. Today we are His reproduction, His many copies, so we should live the same kind of life. (*The Practical Way to Live a Life according to the High Peak of the Divine Revelation in the Holy Scriptures,* p. 25)

Today's Reading

He chose us in eternity past, and one day He regenerated us. He regenerated us on the same day Jesus was born to be the firstborn Son of God in His resurrection (1 Pet. 1:3). In His resurrection we were born to be the many sons of God. This indicates that the firstborn Son is a prototype, and the many sons are the mass reproduction. What should we as the reproduction of the firstborn Son of God be? We should be the God-men. He was the first God-man, the prototype. He was the original copy for xeroxing, and we are the following copies. We should be exactly the same as He is. He is a God-man, and we should be the God-men.

God desired to become a man, and one day He became a man, living on earth as a God-man. Yet when He lived on earth as the God-man, He did not live by His human life, but by His divine life. He was divine. He wanted to become human, and He was human. Yet He lived a human life not by His humanity, but by His divinity. He was a human being that came with divinity. He lived on this earth not only as God but also as man. He lived as a God-man, yet not by the life of man but by the life of God. So His human living was not lived out by the human life but by the divine life. Yet within the divine life, there was the element of humanity, and within the human life, there was the element of divinity. The divine attributes became the human virtues.

First, we need to be clear about the life of Christ, the first God-man, on the earth. He was both God and man, having the divine life and the human life....Christ lived a life of humanity, not by His human life, but by His divine life....He died to live. He was dying every day during His whole life of thirty-three and a half years. He died to Himself that He might live to the Father (John 5:19, 30; 8:28)....I like this phrase *dying to live.* Christ died to Himself in order to live out the divine attributes as His human virtues.

Christ was under the cross all the time on the earth, expressing not Himself but the Father....[John 14:8-10] shows that He was the expression of the Father. Christ lived a life under the cross all the time until He was practically crucified on the cross to accomplish His all-inclusive death for God's eternal redemption of His chosen people. God's chosen people became fallen and lost, but He redeemed them back through the wonderful death of that wonderful Person, Christ. (*The Practical Way to Live a Life according to the High Peak of the Divine Revelation in the Holy Scriptures,* pp. 24-27)

Further Reading: The Practical Way to Live a Life according to the High Peak of the Divine Revelation in the Holy Scriptures, ch. 2

Enlightenment and inspiration: _____

_____

Morning Nourishment

1 Pet. For to this you were called, because Christ also
2:21 suffered on your behalf, leaving you a model so
that you may follow in His steps.

Matt. Then Jesus said to His disciples, If anyone wants
16:24 to come after Me, let him deny himself and take
up his cross and follow Me.

2 Cor. And He died for all that those who live may no
5:15 longer live to themselves but to Him who died for
them and has been raised.

Gal. For I through law have died to law that I might
2:19 live to God.

Intrinsically speaking, to follow Jesus is to be a xerox copy of that first God-man. To follow Jesus is to live the life of a God-man, not by the human life but by the divine life, so that God may be expressed or manifested in the flesh in all His divine attributes becoming the human virtues. This is the intrinsic significance of what it is to follow Christ. So the practical way to live a life according to the high peak of the divine revelation is that you must be a God-man. As a God-man you need to live a life not by yourself but by another One, not by your human life but by His divine life, not to express yourself but to express His divinity in His divine attributes which all become your human virtues. (*The Practical Way to Live a Life according to the High Peak of the Divine Revelation in the Holy Scriptures*, pp. 25-26)

Today's Reading

First Peter 2:21 says that Christ as the first God-man was a model for us. We need to live a life which is a copy, a reproduction, of the life of Christ.

In Matthew 16:24 the Lord said, "If anyone wants to come after Me, let him deny himself and take up his cross and follow Me." This is to live a life of bearing the cross in the steps of Christ (1 Pet. 2:21b).

Both 2 Corinthians 5:15 and Galatians 2:19 show that the believers in Christ should die to themselves and live to God.

Paul said that he was crucified with Christ (Gal. 2:20) to be conformed to His death by the power of His resurrection (Phil. 3:10).

Romans 8:13 says, "For if you live according to the flesh, you must die, but if by the Spirit you put to death the practices of the body, you will live." You have to put to death by the Spirit in His resurrection whatever your body does. This is to be conformed to the death of Christ by the power of His resurrection. No one in his natural life can put everything that his body does to death. But we, the God-men, who are the reproduction of the prototype, can. We can know Him and the power of His resurrection and the fellowship of His sufferings, being conformed to His death.

Such a life of dying to ourselves and living to God is for Christ, the first God-man, to be formed in His many brothers, the many God-men, for the building up of His organic Body that the eternal economy of God might be carried out. The Christian life is not a matter of outwardly loving people or of being meek or patient in our human ethics. We need to die every day (1 Cor. 15:31). The married saints need to die to their spouse. The students need to die to their classmates and teachers. We need to die to live so that the many God-men can become the building material for the building up of the Body of Christ to carry out God's eternal economy.

Thus, a number (not all) of His brothers, the many God-men, through His death and in His resurrection may be constituted to be His overcomers to close this age and to bring in His kingdom age. This is the real meaning of our being a Christian. It is a life of dying every day. We must admit that we have not been that absolute or faithful in practicing this dying-to-live life. God has opened up to us the high peak of His divine revelation. He also puts us in an environment of sufferings to force us to die to live. I hope we all would be brought into the reality of Philippians 3:10: "To know Him and the power of His resurrection and the fellowship of His sufferings, being conformed to His death." (*The Practical Way to Live a Life according to the High Peak of the Divine Revelation in the Holy Scriptures*, pp. 27-29)

Further Reading: The Practical Way to Live a Life according to the High Peak of the Divine Revelation in the Holy Scriptures, ch. 2

Enlightenment and inspiration: _____

_____

Morning Nourishment

Phil. To know Him and the power of His resurrection
3:10 and the fellowship of His sufferings, being conformed to His death.

Rom. Knowing this, that our old man has been crucified
6:6 with *Him* in order that the body of sin might be
annulled, that we should no longer serve sin as slaves.

1 Cor. I protest by the boasting in you, brothers, which I
15:31 have in Christ Jesus our Lord, I die daily.

Now let us see the proper living of a God-man who pursues
Christ. Paul referred to this in the book of Philippians. He wrote to
the church in Philippi, referring to his life of living Christ to magnify
Him, of pursuing Christ to gain Him, and of taking Christ as
the secret of his contentment. In such an Epistle with experiencing Christ as its subject, we can find out that the first thing
in the proper living of a Christ-pursuing God-man is to pursue
to know Christ. In Philippians 3:10a Paul said, "To know Him
[Christ]." Christ is unlimited, and His riches are unsearchable
(Eph. 3:8). Our knowledge of Christ is, on the one hand, by
revelation and, on the other hand, by experience. In these last
forty years most of my messages have been centered on Christ.
I searched out from the holy Scriptures all the items concerning
Christ in the types, Christ in the prophecies, and Christ in plain
words. However, we still need to increase our pursuing of Christ
that we may apprehend with all the saints the dimensions—the
breadth, the length, the height, and the depth—of Christ. Christ
is exceedingly rich; He is all-inclusive and all-extensive. We
need to pursue to know Him. (*A General Outline of God's
Economy and the Proper Living of a God-man*, p. 36)

Today's Reading

The Lord Jesus told us, "If anyone wants to come after Me,
let him deny himself and take up his cross and follow Me" (Matt.
16:24). To deny the self is to take up the cross. When the Lord
Jesus was on the earth, He lived a crucified life daily. Although
He was holy and without sin, He still denied Himself by putting

Himself to death that God might live in Him and be lived out of Him.

Christ took up His cross daily by dying to Himself. Likewise, as God-men who pursue Him, we should bear the cross and live under the cross daily. This means that we should put our natural life on the cross by daily dying to our self and putting to death all the practices of our natural man and our flesh.... This kind of living requires our pursuit. A God-man is one who lives under the cross daily. Hence, to have merely the teaching of the cross is not enough; the cross must become our experience.

Such a living in the shadow of the cross touches the deepest part of our being and every detail in our life. We all know that we need to be careful when we talk to others. We brothers who are married, however, realize that we become very careless when we are talking to our wife. If we are those who live in the shadow of the cross, even our talking to our wife needs to be checked. Are we under the death of the cross when we talk to our wife in a certain way? If we are willing to check in this way, we will see that ninety-nine percent of the things which we say to our wife should never be said. They are things which we speak out of ourself; they are not spoken by the indwelling God in us, but by our natural man. It may be that we do not criticize, judge, or condemn others; instead, we speak nice things about others. But is it Christ who speaks, or is it we who speak? We have to admit that most of the things we say are by ourself without passing through the cross.... We should not speak but allow the Lord to speak. If we truly have this experience, regardless of what we say, we have the cross checking in us: "Is this spoken through the cross? Is the mold of the cross here?"

We are those who belong to Christ; in other words, we are God-men. Therefore, we should live under the death of the cross in all things. It is in this way that the resurrected Lord can manifest His power from within us. (*A General Outline of God's Economy and the Proper Living of a God-man*, pp. 38-40)

Further Reading: A General Outline of God's Economy and the Proper Living of a God-man, ch. 4

Enlightenment and inspiration: _____

_____

Morning Nourishment

**Phil. *Doing* nothing by way of selfish ambition nor by
2:3-4 way of vainglory, but in lowliness of mind considering one another more excellent than yourselves; not regarding each his own virtues, but
each the virtues of others also.
21 For all seek their own things, not the things of
Christ Jesus.
3:3 For we are the circumcision, the ones who serve
by the Spirit of God and boast in Christ Jesus and
have no confidence in the flesh.**

In Philippians 2:3 Paul exhorts the saints to do "nothing by
way of selfish ambition nor by way of vainglory, but in lowliness
of mind considering one another more excellent than yourselves."
Do not think that in the church today there is no selfish ambition
for vainglory. When a brother hears a certain person ministering
the Word in a rich way, he may say to himself, "Wait for a few
years, and I will surprise you with my rich speaking. My speaking
will be much better than this." This is an example of the selfish
ambition for vainglory which may be hidden within you.

In 2:4 Paul goes on to say, "Not regarding each his own
virtues, but each the virtues of others also."…We should not
regard only our own virtues and qualities, but those of others
also. Instead of thinking so much about our own virtues, qualities, abilities, and attainments, we should regard those of
others. In keeping with Paul's word, we should even consider
others more excellent than ourselves. As we consider others in
the church, we should think of them as better than ourselves.
(*The Secret of Experiencing Christ*, p. 108)

Today's Reading

In Philippians 2:21 Paul says that "all seek their own things,
not the things of Christ Jesus." The phrase "their own things"
here refers not to virtues and qualities as in 2:4, but to our
personal affairs. We may care for our personal affairs and not
for the things of Christ. Probably you have not realized that

personal affairs are a negative thing keeping you from the experience of Christ. However, you may actually care more for your domestic affairs than for Christ, more for your education or employment than for the church life. But of Timothy Paul could say that he would "genuinely care for what concerns" the church, whereas others cared for their own things, not the things of Christ. If we go on caring for our own things instead of caring for the things of Christ, there will be no way to have the church life.

In 3:2 Paul issues a serious charge: "Beware of the dogs, beware of the evil workers, beware of the concision." Those who were dogs, evil workers, the concision, held to certain religious concepts which were troubling to the saints and were a source of distraction from Christ. In dealing with such people we should care for one basic principle: Does this person's word help us to experience Christ and to have more of the church life, or does it distract us from Christ and the church? If it does not encourage us to experience Christ and to live the church life, we should pay no attention to it. That person must be a dog, an evil worker, one who contemptuously follows certain religious rituals (the meaning of the term concision)....[Such a] one who should be avoided.

In 3:4-8 Paul goes on to deal with yet another negative thing—confidence in the flesh....In these verses confidence in the flesh refers to all the good items or qualities we have in the flesh. For Paul, these included circumcision on the eighth day and being a Hebrew of the Hebrews. For us today, they may include pride in our nationality or culture. Such confidence in the flesh keeps us from Christ and frustrates the church life.

The last of the negative things in Philippians is what Paul describes as lack (4:11). To be lacking is to have a material need. Being short of the supply to meet a material or financial need may be a cause of serious concern. Such circumstances certainly are a negative thing which needs to be overcome. (*The Secret of Experiencing Christ*, pp. 109-111)

Further Reading: The Secret of Experiencing Christ, ch. 10; *A General Outline of God's Economy and the Proper Living of a God-man*, ch. 4

Enlightenment and inspiration: _____

Morning Nourishment

1 Thes. 5:17 Unceasingly pray.

Rom. 10:12 For there is no distinction between Jew and Greek, for the same Lord *is Lord* of all *and* rich to all who call upon Him;

13 For "whoever calls upon the name of the Lord shall be saved."

Phil. 1:21 For to me, to live is Christ...

In 1 Thessalonians 5:17 Paul charges us to unceasingly pray. What does it mean to pray unceasingly? Although we may eat several meals a day and although we may drink many times during the day, no one can eat and drink without ceasing. But we certainly breathe unceasingly. Paul's command to pray without ceasing implies that unceasing prayer is like breathing. But how can our prayer become our spiritual breathing? How can we turn prayer into breathing? The way to do this is to call on the name of the Lord. We need to call on the Lord Jesus continually. This is the way to breathe, to pray without ceasing. Because we are not accustomed to this, we need to practice calling on the Lord's name all the time. To live is to breathe. Spiritually speaking, to breathe is to call on the Lord's name and to pray. By calling on the name of the Lord Jesus, we breathe the Spirit. (*Life-study of Philippians*, p. 298)

Today's Reading

Just as we must breathe in order to live physically, we must breathe spiritually in order to live Christ. The way to breathe spiritually is to call on the name of the Lord. From my experience I have learned that the way to live Christ is to call on Him continually. It is not sufficient simply to pray several times during the day, in the morning, in the afternoon, and at night. If we pray at these times but do not call on the Lord continually, we shall quench the Spirit. All day long, no matter where we are or what we are doing, we need to call on the Lord. Whatever we are doing, we should call on the Lord Jesus. I can testify that even when I speak for the Lord I call on Him and breathe of Him deep within.

Call on the Lord's name in every situation, even when you are about to lose your temper. By calling on the Lord, you will live Christ. However, if you make up your mind not to lose your temper, you will be defeated. Your temper will be worse. Instead of trying to control your temper, turn to the Lord and call on Him. Say, "Lord Jesus, I love You. Lord, I am going to lose my temper. Be one with me in this." If you do this, you will be saved from your temper, and you will live Christ.

To pray without ceasing by calling on the Lord's name is to live Him. By calling on the Lord, we automatically take Him as our life and spontaneously live Him. If we pray, we shall not do things by ourselves, apart from Christ. Instead, by praying without ceasing, we shall live Christ.

Christ is not only our life, but also our breath. Have you ever realized that Christ is your breath? If you breathe Him all the time, you will live Him. After years of groping, I have discovered that the way to live Christ is to breathe Him, and the way to breathe Him is to call on Him without ceasing.

I can testify from my own experience that if I do not call on the Lord, I cannot live. But if I call on Him, everything is fine. Often when you greet a person and ask him how he is, he will answer, "Oh, I'm fine." Actually, for the most part, people are not fine. Only those who call on the Lord Jesus without ceasing can truly say that they are fine. Often we are troubled by little things in our daily life. The car may not start, or a shoelace may break. Such things can be aggravating and make us angry. When you are angry over a car that will not start or over a broken shoelace, can you honestly say that you are fine? I repeat, only those who call on the name of the Lord Jesus truly are fine.

There is no need always to call on the Lord purposely or deliberately. We may call on Him subconsciously, unconsciously, and unintentionally. This is true breathing. Breathing is unintentional. Let us practice to build up a habit of calling on the Lord's name until we call unconsciously and unintentionally. (*Life-study of Philippians,* pp. 299-301)

Further Reading: Life-study of Philippians, msgs. 1-2, 33-34

Enlightenment and inspiration: _____

Morning Nourishment

Phil.   Let your forbearance be known to all men. The
4:5-7   Lord is near. In nothing be anxious, but in everything, by prayer and petition with thanksgiving,
let your requests be made known to God; and the
peace of God, which surpasses every *man's* understanding, will guard your hearts and your
thoughts in Christ Jesus.

When we have problems in our daily life, we do not have to
seek advice from others, because we have a spirit in us and the
Lord as the Spirit dwelling in our spirit is very near to us. We
can ask Him about everything,...for He can talk with us right
within us....The Lord's Word says, "In nothing be anxious, but
in everything, by prayer and petition with thanksgiving, let
your requests be made known to God" (Phil. 4:6). Hence, if you
have some problem, you just need to tell Him. He is right within
you, and He is with you face to face. The Triune God—the
Father, the Son, and the Spirit—is in us not to trouble us but
to be our Paraclete, Comforter, Supporter. I always pray, "O
Lord, now I am going to take a walk. Support me, sustain me,
and strengthen me." This is to drink the Lord. In this way I have
no anxiety. When anxiety comes, you should say, "O Lord, this
anxiety is Yours, not mine; I give it to You because You bear it
for me." Thus, you receive the Lord's element into you and
metabolism will work constantly in you. Consequently, what is
expressed through you outwardly is Christ. This is to live
Christ. Those who do not know this secret consider to live Christ
a difficult thing. Actually, you just need to practice speaking
with the Lord constantly; then spontaneously you will live
Christ. (*The Organic Aspect of God's Salvation,* pp. 54-55)

Today's Reading

[In Philippians 4:5-6], prayer is general with the essence of
worship and fellowship; petition is special for particular needs.
Both our prayer and petition should be accompanied by thanksgiving to the Lord. The English preposition *to* in the phrase "to

God" is the Greek preposition *pros.* This preposition is often translated "with" (John 1:1; Mark 9:19; Matt. 26:55; 2 Cor. 5:8; 1 Cor. 16:6; 1 John 1:2). It denotes motion towards, in the sense of a living union and communion; thus, it implies fellowship. Hence, the meaning of "to God" here is in fellowship with God. John 1:1 uses the preposition *pros* in the phrase "the Word was with *(pros)* God." Such a word conveys the thought of traffic, something going back and forth. It denotes motion toward some object which produces a transaction in the sense of a living union. Based upon this union, there is communion which is a communication or fellowship.

Whenever we pray, making our petition in the proper way, there should be some traffic between us and God. Something from us should move toward God, causing God to respond to us. This moving back and forth is fellowship. This is the proper meaning of the word *fellowship.* Fellowship is actually the dispensing of God for man to receive. The fellowship we have with God, on God's side, is His dispensing, and, on our side, our receiving. He dispenses, and we receive. The more fellowship we have, the more we receive of God through His dispensing.

When we are short of something, we may become anxious. We should not bear this anxiety by ourselves. We should let God know, by making our requests to Him, by prayer and petition with thanksgiving. This is the kind of prayer we should have. We do not need to pray in the way of begging God to do things for us. We should just tell Him what we need, that is, we should let Him know, not keeping anything within ourselves. If we have any worry or anxiety, we should just tell Him. Our letting Him know is our motion toward Him. Then His response is His dispensing, His mingling of Himself with us, even before He answers our request. This mingling of divinity with humanity is the mingling of two entities, the divine entity and the human entity. (*The Experience and Growth in Life,* pp. 97-98)

Further Reading: The Organic Aspect of God's Salvation, ch. 4; *The Experience and Growth in Life,* msg. 15; *Life-study of Philippians,* msg. 27*

Enlightenment and inspiration: _____

_____

Hymns, #631

1 If I'd know Christ's risen power,
   I must ever love the Cross;
Life from death alone arises;
   There's no gain except by loss.

   If no death, no life,
   If no death, no life;
Life from death alone arises;
   If no death, no life.

2 If I'd have Christ formed within me,
   I must breathe my final breath,
Live within the Cross's shadow,
   Put my soul-life e'er to death.

3 If God thru th' Eternal Spirit
   Nail me ever with the Lord;
Only then as death is working
   Will His life thru me be poured.

Composition for prophecy with main point and sub-points: _____

_____

_____

_____

_____

_____

_____

_____

_____

_____

_____

_____

_____

_____

_____

_____

_____

_____

_____

_____

_____

_____

_____

_____

_____

_____

_____

_____

_____

_____

_____

_____

_____

_____

_____

_____

A Man of Prayer—a God-man
Who Is Constituted with Christ
for the One New Man

Scripture Reading: Col. 1:9, 15-18, 27; 2:9, 16-17; 3:1-4, 10-11; 4:2

Day 1 I. **The emphasis on the church being the Body of Christ is on life, whereas the emphasis on the church being the one new man is on the person (1 Cor. 12:12; Eph. 4:4; 2:15; 4:24):**

A. As the Body of Christ, the church needs Christ as its life; as the one new man, the church needs Christ as its person (Col. 3:4; Eph. 3:17a).

B. The goal of the Lord's recovery is to bring forth the one new man (2:15; 4:24; Col. 3:10-11):

1. In His recovery the Lord is bringing forth the one new man with Himself as the life and the person for God's expression (Eph. 3:17-19; Col. 3:4).

2. The one new man will usher in the kingdom of God and bring Christ, the King, back to this earth (Rev. 11:15).

Day 2 II. **In the one new man, there is only one person—the all-inclusive Christ (Col. 2:17; 3:4, 10-11):**

A. The all-inclusive Christ is the center and circumference, the centrality and the universality, of God's purpose and economy (1:15-18).

B. God's intention in His economy is that Christ be everything; therefore, it is crucial for us to see that God wants nothing but Christ and that in the eyes of God nothing counts except Christ (Matt. 17:5; Col. 3:10-11).

C. We need to be infused, saturated, and permeated with the all-inclusive Christ until in our experience He is everything to us (2:16-17).

D. The all-inclusive Christ is in us, but we need to see Him, know Him, be filled with Him, and become absolutely one with Him (1:27; 3:4).

E. As the embodiment of the Triune God, the all-inclusive Christ is the reality of every positive thing in the universe (2:9, 16-17):

  1. Everything we do day by day should remind us of Christ as the reality of that thing and should remind us to contact Christ, to experience Christ, to enjoy Christ, and to have Christ as our everything.

  2. If we follow the practice of taking Christ as the reality of all the material things in our daily life, our living will revolutionized and transformed; it will be full of Christ.

Day 3

F. The record in Joshua 22:10-34 about building another altar shows us that we must avoid division and that to experience and enjoy the all-inclusive Christ we must be one people, one Body, one universal church (1 Cor. 12:12; Eph. 4:3-4).

G. God's ultimate goal in His economy is to gain the one new man constituted with the preeminent, all-inclusive Christ wrought into a corporate people (Col. 3:10-11; 1:18; 2:9, 16-17):

  1. In the one new man Christ is all and in all; we have no place (3:11).

  2. The one new man is just Christ—Christ spreading and Christ enlarged.

Day 4 III. **The way to experience the indwelling Christ, to be constituted with Christ, and to live Christ in the one new man is to pray in a genuine way (1:3, 9; 4:2-3, 12):**

A. We need the kind of prayer that brings us into contact with the Lord—prayer that causes us to be one with Him in our spirit (1 Cor. 6:17; 2 Tim. 4:22).

B. A life of genuine prayer stops our natural being; a life of prayer is a life that revolts and rebels against our natural being:

1. To pray means to realize that we are nothing and that we can do nothing (Mark 9:28-29).

2. Prayer is the real denial of the self; thus, to pray is to deny ourselves (8:34).

3. To pray is actually to declare, "No longer I but Christ" (Gal. 2:20).

Day 5

C. Paul prayed that the saints would "be filled with the full knowledge of His will in all spiritual wisdom and understanding" (Col. 1:9):

1. In this verse the will of God is concerned with the all-inclusive Christ as our portion (v. 12).

2. The will of God is profound in relation to our knowing, experiencing, and living the all-inclusive Christ:

a. God's will for us is that we know Christ, experience Christ, enjoy Christ, live Christ, and have Christ become our life and our person (Phil. 3:7-10; 1:21a; Col. 3:4; Eph. 3:17a).

b. Christ should be our life and our person; this is the will of God.

D. Paul charged the saints to persevere in prayer (Col. 4:2):

1. As we persevere in prayer, the living person of Christ becomes our experience and enjoyment (1:27).

2. Because prayer involves a battle, we need to persevere in prayer.

3. In order to persevere in prayer, we need to exercise our spirit continually, praying at every time in spirit (1 Tim. 4:7; Eph. 6:18).

E. We need to respond to Christ's intercession by seeking the things that are above and by setting our mind on them (Col. 3:1-2):

1. Because Christ is so active for us in the heavens, we should seek the things that are above and set our mind on them.

2. Christ's ministry of intercession in the heavens requires our response; when we seek the things that are above, we respond and correspond to Christ's heavenly ministry.

3. When Christ prays in heaven, we should pray on earth; this means that there is a transmission between the Christ praying in heaven and us praying on earth.

4. Through our prayer, Christ, the Head, is given a way to carry out His administration through His Body (1:18; 2:19; 3:1-2; 4:2).

5. If we seek the things that are above and have one life and living with Christ, we will be wholly occupied with our Master's enterprise (3:1-4).

6. We need to focus our attention on the things above and remain open to the divine transmission from the heavens; then the all-inclusive Christ will be transmitted into us, and we will be constituted with Christ for the one new man.

Morning Nourishment

Col.   When Christ our life is manifested, then you also
3:4   will be manifested with Him in glory.
Eph.   That Christ may make His home in your hearts
3:17   through faith...
4:24   And put on the new man, which was created
        according to God in righteousness and holiness
        of the reality.

First, we must see that the Body is a matter of life, and the new man is a matter of person. Our body has life in it; without life, it is not a body but a corpse. When we speak of the Body, we understand that it has life in it. Thus, the Body is a matter of life. When we speak of one new man, though, it is a matter of person. A man has a person. Today my body does not need a person; my body only needs life. In other words, my body needs to be healthy, and health is life....Therefore, the body is a matter of life. The new man, however, is a matter of person. My body cannot plan where it will go, but my person can make a plan. There is a person within me who decides, saying, "This morning this body will go to this place, and this evening this body will go to that place." By this you can see the difference between the person and the life that is in the body. The person makes a decision about where to go, and the body immediately takes action. The Body of Christ is a matter of life, whereas the new man is a matter of person.

Still, you all must know that both the life and the person are Christ. The life in this Body is Christ, and the person in this one new man is also Christ. The church is the Body, and this Body needs Christ to be in it as life. The church is also the one new man, and this one new man needs Christ to be in him as his person. (*One Body, One Spirit, and One New Man,* pp. 55-56)

Today's Reading

The Body is a matter of life, and the new man is a matter of person. The Body is for moving; it is an instrument for action. Thus, it was in one Body that the Lord Jesus reconciled both the Jewish and Gentile believers to God. This reconciliation is a Body matter. In the past we thought that...we were individually saved and individually reconciled to God. This is an erroneous concept. We must see that we who were far off and separated from God were reconciled to God not individually but in a corporate instrument....This instrument is the Body of Christ. In one Body both the Jewish believers and the Gentile believers have been reconciled to God. This shows us that the Body is an instrument used by Christ.

The new man is not for moving; the new man is for decision-making and for living. As a human being you may not move at all, but you still must live. The Body is for moving, and the new man is for living....Ephesians 4:24 says that [the new man] was created according to God in righteousness and holiness. Righteousness and holiness are conditions of our living. Thus, living is entirely a matter of the new man. The new man is for living, and eighty to ninety percent of our living is in making decisions. Therefore, you can see two things: the church as the Body is for moving, and the church as the new man is for living by making decisions. On the one hand, the church is the Body of Christ, and we take Christ as our life to act, to work, and to bear responsibilities. On the other hand, the church is the new man, and we take Christ as our person to make plans and to decide on how we should live. Whether it is the Body or the new man, whether in working and moving or in living and in deciding, everything is corporate; nothing is individual. You must see that your living today is the living of the new man, a corporate living, and your decisions are corporate decisions and not your personal decisions.

We cannot be individualistic....Our living is corporate, and our moving is corporate. In our moving we take Christ as our life, and in our living we take Christ as our person. In the Body, Christ is our life, and in the new man, Christ is our person. In the Body we are members one of another, and in the new man we all have one mouth to speak the same thing. This is the church. (*One Body, One Spirit, and One New Man,* pp. 63-66)

Further Reading: One Body, One Spirit, and One New Man, msgs. 3-8; *Life-study of the New Testament, Conclusion Messages,* msg. 216

Enlightenment and inspiration: _____

_____

Morning Nourishment

Col.   Let no one therefore judge you in eating and in
2:16-17 drinking or in respect of a feast or of a new moon
         or of the Sabbath, which are a shadow of the
         things to come, but the body is of Christ.

In Paul's word about shadows we have a hint as to how we may enjoy Christ in a practical way. Since such things as eating and drinking are shadows of which Christ is the substance and reality, we need to be reminded whenever we eat and drink that the real food and the real drink are Christ. When you eat your food, you should simultaneously eat Christ. When you drink some beverage, you should also drink Christ. As you put on your clothing, you should be reminded that Christ is the real clothing, and you should experience Him as such. As you put on your material clothing, you should also put on Christ. It is easy to enjoy Christ in this way. Whatever we do day by day should remind us of Christ as the reality of that thing. Even our breathing should remind us of the necessity of breathing Christ spiritually.

If we follow the practice of taking Christ as the reality of all the material things in our daily life, our daily walk will be revolutionized and transformed. It will be full of Christ. When we eat and drink, we shall take Christ as our spiritual food and drink. Everything we do will remind us to contact Christ, to enjoy Christ, to experience Christ, and to have Christ as our everything. To practice this day by day is truly to enjoy Christ. (*Life-study of Colossians*, p. 485)

Today's Reading

Many things in our environment of daily living are also shadows of Christ. For example, the food we eat is a shadow, not the real food. The real food is Christ. Christ is also the real drink. The clothing we wear to cover us, to beautify us, and to keep us warm is also a shadow of Christ. Christ is the One who truly covers our nakedness, who keeps us warm, and who imparts beauty to us. Christ is also our true dwelling place and real rest. The houses in which we live are a shadow of Christ as our dwelling place. The rest we enjoy at night is also a figure of Christ as our rest. Even the satisfaction we enjoy after a good meal is not the real satisfaction but a shadow of Christ as the reality of satisfaction.

In verse 16 Paul covers matters related to daily life, weekly life, monthly life, and yearly life. As we have pointed out, eating and drinking are daily, the Sabbaths weekly, the new moons monthly, and the feasts yearly. All the aspects of our living are shadows of Christ. Eating and drinking signify daily satisfaction and strengthening, and the Sabbath signifies weekly completion and rest. Without completion, we cannot enjoy rest. Rest always comes from completion and satisfaction. When you have finished a certain matter and are satisfied with it, you are then able to be at rest. After God completed His work of creation on the sixth day, He enjoyed rest on the seventh day. I can testify that I can enjoy rest only when my work has been completed and I am satisfied with it. Hence, the Sabbath signifies completion and rest on a weekly basis.

A new moon signifies a monthly new beginning with light in darkness. Just as the new moon marked a new beginning in Old Testament times, so Christ affords us a new beginning with light in darkness today. Recently I heard the testimony of a Jewish brother who was saved a few months ago. Before he came to the Lord, he was in darkness, like all unbelieving Jews today. But now Christ is his new moon with light in darkness.

The feasts signify yearly enjoyment and joy. Three times a year, God's chosen people came together for the annual feasts, which were times of enjoyment, of rejoicing together before the Lord. Although the feasts were enjoyable, they were simply shadows of Christ. He is the real food, drink, completion, rest, new moon, and feast. Daily we eat and drink Him, weekly we have completion and rest in Him, monthly we experience a new beginning in Him, and throughout the year He is our joy and enjoyment. Daily, weekly, monthly, and yearly Christ is to us the reality of every positive thing. (*Life-study of Colossians,* pp. 198-199)

Further Reading: Life-study of Colossians, msgs. 15, 24-25, 32, 36, 39, 55

Enlightenment and inspiration: _____

_____

Morning Nourishment

Col. And have put on the new man, which is being
3:10-11 renewed unto full knowledge according to the
image of Him who created him, where there cannot be Greek and Jew, circumcision and uncircumcision, barbarian, Scythian, slave, free man,
but Christ is all and in all.

Eph. Being diligent to keep the oneness of the Spirit in the
4:3-4 uniting bond of peace: one Body and one Spirit...

Moses charged [Reuben, Gad, and the half-tribe of Manasseh]
that they had to fight along with their brothers west of the
Jordan before they could enjoy their inheritance east of the
Jordan (Num. 32:20-22). After these tribes fought along with
their brothers, they were qualified to return to their land to
enjoy their inheritance. This indicates that we cannot enjoy
Christ without the Body. We must be one with the Body in order
to share the inheritance of Christ.

When Reuben, Gad, and the half-tribe of Manasseh returned
to enjoy their inheritance of the land, they built a great altar at the
river Jordan (Josh. 22:10). This offended the other tribes and caused
the children of Israel in Canaan to go up in battle against them
(vv. 11-20).... [This] record in Joshua 22 shows us that no matter
what the situation of God's people might be today, we are not
allowed to set up another altar for the worship of God or for
fellowship with God. In God's economy, among God's people there
should be only one altar, in Jerusalem. All God's people had to go
there to offer their sacrifices to God for their worship and fellowship
with God. This indicates that in the enjoyment of Christ division
must be avoided to the uttermost. Nevertheless, in certain
places the dissenting ones, not caring for the one accord in the
Lord's recovery, have formed divisions by building another altar.

It is very significant that in a portion of the holy Word
concerned with the inheritance of the good land we have a
record about the building of another altar. This account shows
us that we must avoid division. To enjoy the all-inclusive Christ
as the good land, we must be one people, one Body, one universal
church to testify for Christ. (*Life-study of Joshua*, pp. 93-94)

Today's Reading

In the new man "Christ is all and in all" [Col. 3:11]. In the new man there is room only for Christ. He is all the members of the new man and in all the members. He is everything in the new man. Actually, He is the new man, His Body (1 Cor. 12:13). In the new man Christ is the centrality and universality.

The word *all* in Colossians 3:11 refers to all the members who make up the new man. Christ is all these members, and He is in all the members. For this reason, in the church there is no room for us. There is no room for any nationality. As those who are part of the new man, we should not regard ourselves as Chinese, Americans, Germans, or any other nationality. Do not even say that you are so-and-so. Since Christ is all and in all in the new man and you are part of the new man, then you are part of Christ. Each member, each part, of the new man is Christ.

In saying that there cannot be any natural person in the new man, verse 11 is very strong. What a great mistake it is to translate the Greek here as the new self!...According to the context, the new man in 3:10 certainly does not denote the new self, for the new man is made up of believers from many different cultural backgrounds. This is not true of the so-called new self. No doubt, the new man here is a corporate man, the church, Christ's Body. Although many different kinds of people make up the church, all are part of Christ. They are no longer the natural person. Christ is everyone in the new man, and He is in everyone in the new man. What a tremendous vision it is to see that Christ is all and in all!

It is crucial for us to see two things: that we need to be renewed unto full knowledge according to the all-inclusive Christ, who is the image of God; and that in the church as the new man Christ is everyone and in everyone. In the church, the new man, there is nothing but Christ. (*Life-study of Colossians,* pp. 237-238)

Further Reading: Life-study of Joshua, msg. 14; *Life-study of Colossians,* msgs. 28, 30*

Enlightenment and inspiration: _____

_____

Morning Nourishment

Col. 1:3 We give thanks to God, the Father of our Lord
Jesus Christ, praying always concerning you.
1 Cor. 6:17 But he who is joined to the Lord is one spirit.
2 Tim. 4:22 The Lord be with your spirit. Grace be with you.

Often when we pray, we do not enter into genuine prayer.
Through experience we can differentiate or discern prayer that
is genuine from prayer that is not genuine. Do you know why
it is so difficult to pray in a genuine way? The main hindrance
is not sin or worldliness; it is cultural opinion. Unconsciously
and subconsciously, we are still controlled by our cultural
opinions. However, if we persevere in prayer, we shall eventually pray in a genuine way. This means that in our prayer we
are released from cultural opinions and enter into the spirit.
Whenever we experience genuine prayer, we are outside of our
culture; in particular, we are outside of our cultural opinion.
During times of genuine prayer, we are in our spirit, and we are
one spirit with the Lord. It is at these times that we live Christ.

Furthermore, at such times of genuine prayer the death of
Christ works within us in a prevailing way to terminate all the
negative things in our being. Spontaneously, Christ's resurrection power also prevails in us. As a result, we are actually one
with Christ and identified with Him. This experience during
times of genuine prayer gives us a taste of the normal Christian
life. (*Life-study of Colossians,* p. 279)

Today's Reading

To pray perseveringly means that we should never depart
from the praying spirit. We should remain in a praying condition. To be in this condition is to be out of our opinion and to be
one spirit with the Lord, living Him and taking Him as our life
and as our person. Spontaneously we are away from everything
other than Christ, and we are living by this living Person. Our
problem is that we do not remain in such a condition of prayer.
This is the reason Paul charges us to persevere in prayer. We
must pray perseveringly in order to be preserved in such a

praying condition. In other words, our daily living should be the same as our experience in times of genuine prayer. Our experience in prayer should become a model of our daily Christian life.

In these days we are burdened to look to the Lord that we may see the true significance of living Christ. We thank Him that gradually He is showing us what it means to live Him. One aspect of living Christ is that of remaining in a praying condition. When we are in this condition, we are outside of culture. Because we are one spirit with this living Person, taking Him as our life and as our person, there is no striving to live properly. Rather, as we are one with the Lord in spirit, the death of Christ is applied to us, and His resurrection power becomes prevailing in us. Then we spontaneously live Him.

If we would experience Christ and live Him, we need to remain in an atmosphere of prayer. Many of us can testify that by prayer we are brought into the spirit, where we are one with the Lord and take Him as our life. This experience is so precious that when we are enjoying it, we do not want it to end. We like to remain in spirit to be one with the Lord. However, as soon as our time of prayer is over, most of the time we revert to our natural way of living. We are no longer in an atmosphere of prayer. Automatically we begin to try once again to be holy, spiritual, and victorious. Whenever we fail, we repent, confess to the Lord, and resolve to try again. This is not the way to live the Christian life. On the contrary, our daily living should be the same as our experience in genuine prayer. When we pray ourselves into the spirit, we are one with the Lord, we enjoy His presence, and we spontaneously live Him. Without exerting any effort, we are holy, spiritual, and victorious. We have no problems and no anxieties. I believe we all have had experiences like this in prayer....This is what it means to live Christ. (*Life-study of Colossians,* pp. 280, 334-335)

Further Reading: Life-study of Colossians, msgs. 33, 39, 55; *Life-study of Mark,* msg. 27

Enlightenment and inspiration: _____

_____
_____
_____

Morning Nourishment

Col. Persevere in prayer, watching in it with thanks-
4:2 giving.
1 Tim. But the profane and old-womanish myths refuse,
4:7 and exercise yourself unto godliness.
Eph. By means of all prayer and petition, praying at
6:18 every time in spirit and watching unto this in all
      perseverance and petition concerning all the saints.

In Colossians 4:2 Paul tells us to persevere in prayer. It is not Paul's intention that we forget all the practical necessities of daily life and simply give ourselves to prayer. He means that we should pray in order to live Christ in all that we do day by day. As we have said, we should pray as we are about to talk with our husband or wife or with our children. In such prayer we may say, "Lord, I am one with You, and You are one with me. Lord, I am about to speak to my children. Lord, will You take the lead in this matter?" This is to persevere in prayer, to pray unceasingly.

Actually, living Christ is a matter of praying. If we would live by Christ, we need to pray. If you intend to go shopping, ask the Lord if He is pleased to go with you. As you are about to purchase a certain item, ask the Lord if He is happy about buying that item. Even in the smallest details we need to inquire of the Lord. To do this is to persevere in prayer and thereby to live Christ. The way to live Christ is by praying to Him all day long. (*Life-study of Colossians,* p. 312)

Today's Reading

If we would express Christ in our human living and preserve the grace we have received from the Lord, we need to persevere in prayer. As we spend time to consider the revelation of the all-inclusive Christ in Colossians, we shall surely receive grace from the Lord. Eventually, we shall see that we and Christ are one, that His peace is arbitrating within us, and that His word is filling us. Then we shall be able to live Him out and express Him. However, no matter how much grace we receive from the Lord, it will leak away if we fail to persevere in prayer. Only prayer can maintain the grace we receive. Only through prayer can this grace become prevailing and living in our experience. To be sure, the Christian life is a life of receiving grace. But this life needs to be sustained by prayer.

In 4:2 Paul charges us to persevere in prayer. This means that we should not merely continue in prayer, but we should strive to continue. Almost everything in our environment is contrary to prayer. In order to pray, we must go against the tide, the current, of our environment. If we fail to pray, we shall be swept downstream. Only prayer can enable us to go against the current. Therefore, we need to persevere in prayer, to pray persistently.

Day by day we need to exercise ourselves to pray. We should even set aside certain times each day for prayer. Do not excuse yourself by saying that you do not have the burden to pray. Pray even when you seem to have no burden, or when apparently you have nothing to say to the Lord. You have much to say to others. Why not go to the Lord and tell Him the very things you tell them? If you do not know what to say to the Lord, pray like this: "Lord, I come to You, but I don't know what to say, and I don't know how to pray. Lord, teach me to pray and tell me what to say. Lord, in this matter have mercy on me." If you do this, you will find that often when you pray in this way, some genuine prayer will come forth. When you feel that you are burdened to pray, your prayer may not be genuine. But when you go to the Lord in prayer even without a burden, telling Him that you have nothing to say, you will find yourself refreshed in the Lord and able to pray genuinely. When we open to the Lord and admit that we do not know what to say to Him, we breathe in fresh spiritual air, and we are preserved in the Lord's grace.

Paul also encourages us to watch in prayer. We need to be watchful against the enemy. We do not know what will happen in the next few minutes. We need to be watchful because the Christian life is a life of fighting, a life of warfare. (*Life-study of Colossians,* pp. 252-254)

Further Reading: Life-study of Colossians, msgs. 3, 30, 36, 48, 57

Enlightenment and inspiration: _____

_____

_____

Morning Nourishment

Col. If therefore you were raised together with Christ,
3:1-2 seek the things which are above, where Christ is,
sitting at the right hand of God. Set your mind on
the things which are above, not on the things
which are on the earth.

4:3 Praying at the same time for us also, that God would
open to us a door for the word, to speak the mystery of Christ (because of which also I am bound).

12 Epaphras, who is one of you, a slave of Christ
Jesus, greets you, always struggling on your behalf in his prayers that you may stand mature and
fully assured in all the will of God.

We need to be those who respond to Christ's heavenly
ministry. For centuries, Christ has tried without adequate
success to get a people to respond to His ministry in the heavens.
By His mercy and grace, there is on earth today a group of people
in the Lord's recovery responding to Christ's heavenly ministry.
Let us be those who tell the Lord that we are one with Him in
this ministry. Day and night, we need to respond to the Christ
who is above all. When I respond to the Lord, saying, "Amen,
Lord," I have the conviction deep within that Christ is interceding and ministering, that He is transmitting His riches into me
and infusing me with the element of God. Because of this
transmission and infusion, I am filled and stirred for the Lord's
interests. Sometimes I am so beside myself with joy that I
hardly know what to do. This is what it means to seek the things
above. (*Life-study of Colossians*, p. 547)

Today's Reading

If we seek the things above and have one living with Christ,
we shall be wholly occupied with the enterprise of our Master.
Our heart will be with Him in heaven, where He is interceding
for the churches, supplying the saints, and administrating
God's government. This will be our concern, our desire. If we
take Christ as life and seek the things which are above in such

a way, the lustful members will be put to death, the evil elements in the fallen soul will be put away, and the old man will be put off. Furthermore, we shall automatically put on the new man.

To us, Colossians should not be only a book of doctrine, but should be a book of experience. Although the Christ revealed in this book is profound, extensive, and all-inclusive, we can still experience Him. We can enjoy Him as our daily necessities, take Him as our life, and live together with Him. Furthermore, we can seek the things which are above and set our mind on them. Do you not aspire to be one with the Lord in the heavenlies and to have a heart that is one with His heart? Do you not long to be one with Him in His priesthood, ministry, and administration? I would encourage all the young people especially to care for God's purpose by seeking the things which are above and living together with Christ.

It is wonderful to enjoy Christ as the reality of our daily necessities, but it is even more wonderful to take Him as our life and live together with Him. I can testify that the more we live Christ and take His concern as our concern, the happier we are. My only concern is the Lord's recovery with all the churches and all the saints. My desire is that the saints would experience Christ and grow in life. I have no other burden, no other concern. I am fully occupied with God's purpose. Because I am filled with Christ's concern, I am very happy. There is no room in me for negative things. Being occupied with the Lord's interests makes me very healthy.

I am happy that there are so many young people in the Lord's recovery. The recovery certainly has a glorious future. We all need to care for the Lord's interests. While He is praying in heaven, we respond in prayer on earth. Thus, we experience the transmission between Christ and us, a transmission that will make us happy and full of joy. Christ works in the heavens, and we work on earth. In this way, we not only enjoy Christ as the reality of our necessities, but we also take Him as our life and have one living with Him. (*Life-study of Colossians,* pp. 534-535)

Further Reading: Life-study of Colossians, msgs. 38, 59-61

Enlightenment and inspiration: _____

_____

Hymns, #538

1   It is God's intent and pleasure
      To have Christ revealed in me,
    Nothing outward as religion,
      But His Christ within to be.

        It is God's intent and pleasure
          That His Christ be wrought in me;
        Nothing outwardly performing,
          But His Christ my all to be.

2   It is God's intent and pleasure
      That His Christ may live in me;
    Nothing as an outward practise,
      But Christ working inwardly.

3   It is God's intent and pleasure
      That His Christ be formed in me;
    Not the outward forms to follow,
      But Christ growing inwardly.

4   It is God's intent and pleasure
      That His Christ make home in me;
    Not just outwardly to serve Him,
      But Christ dwelling inwardly.

5   It is God's intent and pleasure
      That His Christ my hope may be;
    It is not objective glory,
      But 'tis Christ subjectively.

6   It is God's intent and pleasure
      That His Christ be all in me;
    Nothing outwardly possessing,
      But His Christ eternally.

Composition for prophecy with main point and sub-points: _____

_____
_____
_____
_____
_____
_____
_____
_____
_____
_____
_____
_____
_____
_____
_____
_____
_____
_____
_____
_____
_____
_____
_____
_____
_____
_____
_____
_____
_____
_____
_____
_____
_____
_____
_____
_____
_____

Reading Schedule for the Recovery Version of the New Testament with Footnotes

Wk.	Lord's Day	Monday	Tuesday	Wednesday	Thursday	Friday	Saturday
1	☐ Matt 1:1-2	☐ 1:3-7	☐ 1:8-17	☐ 1:18-25	☐ 2:1-23	☐ 3:1-6	☐ 3:7-17
2	☐ 4:1-11	☐ 4:12-25	☐ 5:1-4	☐ 5:5-12	☐ 5:13-20	☐ 5:21-26	☐ 5:27-48
3	☐ 6:1-8	☐ 6:9-18	☐ 6:19-34	☐ 7:1-12	☐ 7:13-29	☐ 8:1-13	☐ 8:14-22
4	☐ 8:23-34	☐ 9:1-13	☐ 9:14-17	☐ 9:18-34	☐ 9:35—10:5	☐ 10:6-25	☐ 10:26-42
5	☐ 11:1-15	☐ 11:16-30	☐ 12:1-14	☐ 12:15-32	☐ 12:33-42	☐ 12:43—13:2	☐ 13:3-12
6	☐ 13:13-30	☐ 13:31-43	☐ 13:44-58	☐ 14:1-13	☐ 14:14-21	☐ 14:22-36	☐ 15:1-20
7	☐ 15:21-31	☐ 15:32-39	☐ 16:1-12	☐ 16:13-20	☐ 16:21-28	☐ 17:1-13	☐ 17:14-27
8	☐ 18:1-14	☐ 18:15-22	☐ 18:23-35	☐ 19:1-15	☐ 19:16-30	☐ 20:1-16	☐ 20:17-34
9	☐ 21:1-11	☐ 21:12-22	☐ 21:23-32	☐ 21:33-46	☐ 22:1-22	☐ 22:23-33	☐ 22:34-46
10	☐ 23:1-12	☐ 23:13-39	☐ 24:1-14	☐ 24:15-31	☐ 24:32-51	☐ 25:1-13	☐ 25:14-30
11	☐ 25:31-46	☐ 26:1-16	☐ 26:17-35	☐ 26:36-46	☐ 26:47-64	☐ 26:65-75	☐ 27:1-26
12	☐ 27:27-44	☐ 27:45-56	☐ 27:57—28:15	☐ 28:16-20	☐ Mark 1:1	☐ 1:2-6	☐ 1:7-13
13	☐ 1:14-28	☐ 1:29-45	☐ 2:1-12	☐ 2:13-28	☐ 3:1-19	☐ 3:20-35	☐ 4:1-25
14	☐ 4:26-41	☐ 5:1-20	☐ 5:21-43	☐ 6:1-29	☐ 6:30-56	☐ 7:1-23	☐ 7:24-37
15	☐ 8:1-26	☐ 8:27—9:1	☐ 9:2-29	☐ 9:30-50	☐ 10:1-16	☐ 10:17-34	☐ 10:35-52
16	☐ 11:1-16	☐ 11:17-33	☐ 12:1-27	☐ 12:28-44	☐ 13:1-13	☐ 13:14-37	☐ 14:1-26
17	☐ 14:27-52	☐ 14:53-72	☐ 15:1-15	☐ 15:16-47	☐ 16:1-8	☐ 16:9-20	☐ Luke 1:1-4
18	☐ 1:5-25	☐ 1:26-46	☐ 1:47-56	☐ 1:57-80	☐ 2:1-8	☐ 2:9-20	☐ 2:21-39
19	☐ 2:40-52	☐ 3:1-20	☐ 3:21-38	☐ 4:1-13	☐ 4:14-30	☐ 4:31-44	☐ 5:1-26
20	☐ 5:27—6:16	☐ 6:17-38	☐ 6:39-49	☐ 7:1-17	☐ 7:18-23	☐ 7:24-35	☐ 7:36-50
21	☐ 8:1-15	☐ 8:16-25	☐ 8:26-39	☐ 8:40-56	☐ 9:1-17	☐ 9:18-26	☐ 9:27-36
22	☐ 9:37-50	☐ 9:51-62	☐ 10:1-11	☐ 10:12-24	☐ 10:25-37	☐ 10:38-42	☐ 11:1-13
23	☐ 11:14-26	☐ 11:27-36	☐ 11:37-54	☐ 12:1-12	☐ 12:13-21	☐ 12:22-34	☐ 12:35-48
24	☐ 12:49-59	☐ 13:1-9	☐ 13:10-17	☐ 13:18-30	☐ 13:31—14:6	☐ 14:7-14	☐ 14:15-24
25	☐ 14:25-35	☐ 15:1-10	☐ 15:11-21	☐ 15:22-32	☐ 16:1-13	☐ 16:14-22	☐ 16:23-31
26	☐ 17:1-19	☐ 17:20-37	☐ 18:1-14	☐ 18:15-30	☐ 18:31-43	☐ 19:1-10	☐ 19:11-27

Reading Schedule for the Recovery Version of the New Testament with Footnotes

Wk.	Lord's Day	Monday	Tuesday	Wednesday	Thursday	Friday	Saturday
27	□ Luke 19:28-48	□ 20:1-19	□ 20:20-38	□ 20:39—21:4	□ 21:5-27	□ 21:28-38	□ 22:1-20
28	□ 22:21-38	□ 22:39-54	□ 22:55-71	□ 23:1-43	□ 23:44-56	□ 24:1-12	□ 24:13-35
29	□ 24:36-53	□ John 1:1-13	□ 1:14-18	□ 1:19-34	□ 1:35-51	□ 2:1-11	□ 2:12-22
30	□ 2:23—3:13	□ 3:14-21	□ 3:22-36	□ 4:1-14	□ 4:15-26	□ 4:27-42	□ 4:43-54
31	□ 5:1-16	□ 5:17-30	□ 5:31-47	□ 6:1-15	□ 6:16-31	□ 6:32-51	□ 6:52-71
32	□ 7:1-9	□ 7:10-24	□ 7:25-36	□ 7:37-52	□ 7:53—8:11	□ 8:12-27	□ 8:28-44
33	□ 8:45-59	□ 9:1-13	□ 9:14-34	□ 9:35—10:9	□ 10:10-30	□ 10:31—11:4	□ 11:5-22
34	□ 11:23-40	□ 11:41-57	□ 12:1-11	□ 12:12-24	□ 12:25-36	□ 12:37-50	□ 13:1-11
35	□ 13:12-30	□ 13:31-38	□ 14:1-6	□ 14:7-20	□ 14:21-31	□ 15:1-11	□ 15:12-27
36	□ 16:1-15	□ 16:16-33	□ 17:1-5	□ 17:6-13	□ 17:14-24	□ 17:25—18:11	□ 18:12-27
37	□ 18:28-40	□ 19:1-16	□ 19:17-30	□ 19:31-42	□ 20:1-13	□ 20:14-18	□ 20:19-22
38	□ 20:23-31	□ 21:1-14	□ 21:15-22	□ 21:23-25	□ Acts 1:1-8	□ 1:9-14	□ 1:15-26
39	□ 2:1-13	□ 2:14-21	□ 2:22-36	□ 2:37-41	□ 2:42-47	□ 3:1-18	□ 3:19—4:22
40	□ 4:23-37	□ 5:1-16	□ 5:17-32	□ 5:33-42	□ 6:1—7:1	□ 7:2-29	□ 7:30-60
41	□ 8:1-13	□ 8:14-25	□ 8:26-40	□ 9:1-19	□ 9:20-43	□ 10:1-16	□ 10:17-33
42	□ 10:34-48	□ 11:1-18	□ 11:19-30	□ 12:1-25	□ 13:1-12	□ 13:13-43	□ 13:44—14:5
43	□ 14:6-28	□ 15:1-12	□ 15:13-34	□ 15:35—16:5	□ 16:6-18	□ 16:19-40	□ 17:1-18
44	□ 17:19-34	□ 18:1-17	□ 18:18-28	□ 19:1-20	□ 19:21-41	□ 20:1-12	□ 20:13-38
45	□ 21:1-14	□ 21:15-26	□ 21:27-40	□ 22:1-21	□ 22:22-29	□ 22:30—23:11	□ 23:12-15
46	□ 23:16-30	□ 23:31—24:21	□ 24:22—25:5	□ 25:6-27	□ 26:1-13	□ 26:14-32	□ 27:1-26
47	□ 27:27—28:10	□ 28:11-22	□ 28:23-31	□ Rom 1:1-2	□ 1:3-7	□ 1:8-17	□ 1:18-25
48	□ 1:26—2:10	□ 2:11-29	□ 3:1-20	□ 3:21-31	□ 4:1-12	□ 4:13-25	□ 5:1-11
49	□ 5:12-17	□ 5:18—6:5	□ 6:6-11	□ 6:12-23	□ 7:1-12	□ 7:13-25	□ 8:1-2
50	□ 8:3-6	□ 8:7-13	□ 8:14-25	□ 8:26-39	□ 9:1-18	□ 9:19—10:3	□ 10:4-15
51	□ 10:16—11:10	□ 11:11-22	□ 11:23-36	□ 12:1-3	□ 12:4-21	□ 13:1-14	□ 14:1-12
52	□ 14:13-23	□ 15:1-13	□ 15:14-33	□ 16:1-5	□ 16:6-24	□ 16:25-27	□ I Cor 1:1-4

Reading Schedule for the Recovery Version of the New Testament with Footnotes

Wk.	Lord's Day	Monday	Tuesday	Wednesday	Thursday	Friday	Saturday
53	I Cor 1:5-9	1:10-17	1:18-31	2:1-5	2:6-10	2:11-16	3:1-9
54	3:10-13	3:14-23	4:1-9	4:10-21	5:1-13	6:1-11	6:12-20
55	7:1-16	7:17-24	7:25-40	8:1-13	9:1-15	9:16-27	10:1-4
56	10:5-13	10:14-33	11:1-6	11:7-16	11:17-26	11:27-34	12:1-11
57	12:12-22	12:23-31	13:1-13	14:1-12	14:13-25	14:26-33	14:34-40
58	15:1-19	15:20-28	15:29-34	15:35-49	15:50-58	16:1-9	16:10-24
59	II Cor 1:1-4	1:5-14	1:15-22	1:23—2:11	2:12-17	3:1-6	3:7-11
60	3:12-18	4:1-6	4:7-12	4:13-18	5:1-8	5:9-15	5:16-21
61	6:1-13	6:14—7:4	7:5-16	8:1-15	8:16-24	9:1-15	10:1-6
62	10:7-18	11:1-15	11:16-33	12:1-10	12:11-21	13:1-10	13:11-14
63	Gal 1:1-5	1:6-14	1:15-24	2:1-13	2:14-21	3:1-4	3:5-14
64	3:15-22	3:23-29	4:1-7	4:8-20	4:21-31	5:1-12	5:13-21
65	5:22-26	6:1-10	6:11-15	6:16-18	Eph 1:1-3	1:4-6	1:7-10
66	1:11-14	1:15-18	1:19-23	2:1-5	2:6-10	2:11-14	2:15-18
67	2:19-22	3:1-7	3:8-13	3:14-18	3:19-21	4:1-4	4:5-10
68	4:11-16	4:17-24	4:25-32	5:1-10	5:11-21	5:22-26	5:27-33
69	6:1-9	6:10-14	6:15-18	6:19-24	Phil 1:1-7	1:8-18	1:19-26
70	1:27—2:4	2:5-11	2:12-16	2:17-30	3:1-6	3:7-11	3:12-16
71	3:17-21	4:1-9	4:10-23	Col 1:1-8	1:9-13	1:14-23	1:24-29
72	2:1-7	2:8-15	2:16-23	3:1-4	3:5-15	3:16-25	4:1-18
73	I Thes 1:1-3	1:4-10	2:1-12	2:13—3:5	3:6-13	4:1-10	4:11—5:11
74	5:12-28	II Thes 1:1-12	2:1-17	3:1-18	I Tim 1:1-2	1:3-4	1:5-14
75	1:15-20	2:1-7	2:8-15	3:1-13	3:14—4:5	4:6-16	5:1-25
76	6:1-10	6:11-21	II Tim 1:1-10	1:11-18	2:1-15	2:16-26	3:1-13
77	3:14—4:8	4:9-22	Titus 1:1-4	1:5-16	2:1-15	3:1-8	3:9-15

Reading Schedule for the Recovery Version of the New Testament with Footnotes

Wk.	Lord's Day	Monday	Tuesday	Wednesday	Thursday	Friday	Saturday
79	☐ Heb 3:1-6	☐ 3:7-19	☐ 4:1-9	☐ 4:10-13	☐ 4:14-16	☐ 5:1-10	☐ 5:11—6:3
80	☐ 6:4-8	☐ 6:9-20	☐ 7:1-10	☐ 7:11-28	☐ 8:1-6	☐ 8:7-13	☐ 9:1-4
81	☐ 9:5-14	☐ 9:15-28	☐ 10:1-18	☐ 10:19-28	☐ 10:29-39	☐ 11:1-6	☐ 11:7-19
82	☐ 11:20-31	☐ 11:32-40	☐ 12:1-2	☐ 12:3-13	☐ 12:14-17	☐ 12:18-26	☐ 12:27-29
83	☐ 13:1-7	☐ 13:8-12	☐ 13:13-15	☐ 13:16-25	☐ James1:1-8	☐ 1:9-18	☐ 1:19-27
84	☐ 2:1-13	☐ 2:14-26	☐ 3:1-18	☐ 4:1-10	☐ 4:11-17	☐ 5:1-12	☐ 5:13-20
85	☐ I Pet 1:1-2	☐ 1:3-4	☐ 1:5	☐ 1:6-9	☐ 1:10-12	☐ 1:13-17	☐ 1:18-25
86	☐ 2:1-3	☐ 2:4-8	☐ 2:9-17	☐ 2:18-25	☐ 3:1-13	☐ 3:14-22	☐ 4:1-6
87	☐ 4:7-16	☐ 4:17-19	☐ 5:1-4	☐ 5:5-9	☐ 5:10-14	☐ II Pet 1:1-2	☐ 1:3-4
88	☐ 1:5-8	☐ 1:9-11	☐ 1:12-18	☐ 1:19-21	☐ 2:1-3	☐ 2:4-11	☐ 2:12-22
89	☐ 3:1-6	☐ 3:7-9	☐ 3:10-12	☐ 3:13-15	☐ 3:16	☐ 3:17-18	☐ I John 1:1-2
90	☐ 1:3-4	☐ 1:5	☐ 1:6	☐ 1:7	☐ 1:8-10	☐ 2:1-2	☐ 2:3-11
91	☐ 2:12-14	☐ 2:15-19	☐ 2:20-23	☐ 2:24-27	☐ 2:28-29	☐ 3:1-5	☐ 3:6-10
92	☐ 3:11-18	☐ 3:19-24	☐ 4:1-6	☐ 4:7-11	☐ 4:12-15	☐ 4:16—5:3	☐ 5:4-13
93	☐ 5:14-17	☐ 5:18-21	☐ II John 1:1-3	☐ 1:4-9	☐ 1:10-13	☐ III John 1:1-6	☐ 1:7-14
94	☐ Jude 1:1-4	☐ 1:5-10	☐ 1:11-19	☐ 1:20-25	☐ Rev 1:1-3	☐ 1:4-6	☐ 1:7-11
95	☐ 1:12-13	☐ 1:14-16	☐ 1:17-20	☐ 2:1-6	☐ 2:7	☐ 2:8-9	☐ 2:10-11
96	☐ 2:12-14	☐ 2:15-17	☐ 2:18-23	☐ 2:24-29	☐ 3:1-3	☐ 3:4-6	☐ 3:7-9
97	☐ 3:10-13	☐ 3:14-18	☐ 3:19-22	☐ 4:1-5	☐ 4:6-7	☐ 4:8-11	☐ 5:1-6
98	☐ 5:7-14	☐ 6:1-8	☐ 6:9-17	☐ 7:1-8	☐ 7:9-17	☐ 8:1-6	☐ 8:7-12
99	☐ 8:13—9:11	☐ 9:12-21	☐ 10:1-4	☐ 10:5-11	☐ 11:1-4	☐ 11:5-14	☐ 11:15-19
100	☐ 12:1-4	☐ 12:5-9	☐ 12:10-18	☐ 13:1-10	☐ 13:11-18	☐ 14:1-5	☐ 14:6-12
101	☐ 14:13-20	☐ 15:1-8	☐ 16:1-12	☐ 16:13-21	☐ 17:1-6	☐ 17:7-18	☐ 18:1-8
102	☐ 18:9—19:4	☐ 19:5-10	☐ 19:11-16	☐ 19:17-21	☐ 20:1-6	☐ 20:7-10	☐ 20:11-15
103	☐ 21:1	☐ 21:2	☐ 21:3-8	☐ 21:9-13	☐ 21:14-18	☐ 21:19-21	☐ 21:22-27
104	☐ 22:1	☐ 22:2	☐ 22:3-11	☐ 22:12-15	☐ 22:16-17	☐ 22:18-21	☐

Week 1 — Day 4 — Today's verses

John 14:30 I will no longer speak much with you, for the ruler of the world is coming, and in Me he has nothing.

17:1 These things Jesus spoke, and lifting up His eyes to heaven, He said, Father, the hour has come; glorify Your Son that the Son may glorify You.

1 Pet. 2:23 ...Suffering, He did not threaten but kept committing all to Him who judges righteously.

Luke 23:46 And crying with a loud voice, Jesus said, Father, into Your hands I commit My spirit....

_____
Date

Week 1 — Day 5 — Today's verses

Rom. 8:26-27 Moreover, in like manner the Spirit also joins in to help us in our weakness, for we do not know for what we should pray as is fitting, but the Spirit Himself intercedes for us with groanings which cannot be uttered. But He who searches the hearts knows what the mind of the Spirit is, because He intercedes for the saints according to God.

James 5:17 Elijah was a man of like feeling with us, and he earnestly prayed that it would not rain; and it did not rain on the earth for three years and six months.

Eph. 6:18 By means of all prayer and petition, praying at every time in spirit...

_____
Date

Week 1 — Day 6 — Today's verses

John 17:17 Sanctify them in the truth; Your word is truth.

14:13 And whatever you ask in My name, that I will do, that the Father may be glorified in the Son.

19 Yet a little while and the world beholds Me no longer, but you behold Me; because I live, you also shall live.

Jude 20 But you, beloved, building up yourselves upon your most holy faith, praying in the Holy Spirit.

_____
Date

Week 1 — Day 1 — Today's verses

Hab. 3:2 ...O Jehovah, revive Your work in the midst of the years....

Hosea 6:2 He will enliven us after two days; on the third day He will raise us up, and we will live in His presence.

Rom. 8:29 Because those whom He foreknew, He also predestinated to be conformed to the image of His Son, that He might be the Firstborn among many brothers.

Col. 3:4 When Christ our life is manifested, then you also will be manifested with Him in glory.

_____
Date

Week 1 — Day 2 — Today's verses

Matt. 16:24 Then Jesus said to His disciples, If anyone wants to come after Me, let him deny himself and take up his cross and follow Me.

Gal. 2:20 I am crucified with Christ; and it is no longer I who live, but it is Christ who lives in me; and the life which I now live in the flesh I live in faith, the faith of the Son of God, who loved me and gave Himself up for me.

Phil. 1:21 For to me, to live is Christ...

_____
Date

Week 1 — Day 3 — Today's verses

Luke 5:16 But He Himself often withdrew in the wilderness and prayed.

Matt. 14:23 ...He went up to the mountain privately to pray. And when night fell, He was there alone.

1 Tim. 3:16 And confessedly, great is the mystery of godliness: He who was manifested in the flesh....

John 5:19 ...The Son can do nothing from Himself except what He sees the Father doing; for whatever that One does, these things the Son also does in like manner.

_____
Date

Week 2 — Day 1
Today's verses

Matt. 6:9   You then pray in this way: Our Father who is in the heavens, Your name be sanctified.

Acts 5:41   So they went from the presence of the Sanhedrin, rejoicing that they were counted worthy to be dishonored on behalf of the Name.

Heb. 12:10   ...[God disciplines] for what is profitable that we might partake of His holiness.

Date

Week 2 — Day 2
Today's verses

Matt. 6:10   Your kingdom come; Your will be done, as in heaven, so also on earth.

Rom. 14:17   For the kingdom of God is not eating and drinking, but righteousness and peace and joy in the Holy Spirit.

Date

Week 2 — Day 3
Today's verses

Matt. 6:11-12   Give us today our daily bread. And forgive us our debts, as we also have forgiven our debtors.

34   Therefore do not be anxious for tomorrow, for tomorrow will be anxious for itself; sufficient for the day is its own evil.

Date

Week 2 — Day 4
Today's verses

Matt. 6:13   And do not bring us into temptation, but deliver us from the evil one....

26:41   Watch and pray that you may not enter into temptation....

Eph. 5:16   Redeeming the time, because the days are evil.

Date

Week 2 — Day 5
Today's verses

Matt. 6:5-6   And when you pray, you shall not be like the hypocrites, because they love to pray standing in the synagogues and on the street corners, so that they may be seen by men. Truly I say to you, They have their reward in full. But you, when you pray, enter into your private room, and shut your door and pray to your Father who is in secret; and your Father who sees in secret will repay you.

Date

Week 2 — Day 6
Today's verses

Matt. 6:14-18   For if you forgive men their offenses, your heavenly Father will forgive you also; but if you do not forgive men their offenses, neither will your Father forgive your offenses. And when you fast, do not be like the sullen-faced hypocrites, for they disfigure their faces so that they may appear to men to be fasting. Truly I say to you, They have their reward in full. But you, when you fast, anoint your head and wash your face, so that you may not appear to men to be fasting, but to your Father who is in secret; and your Father who sees in secret will repay you.

Date

Week 3 — Day 6 — Today's verses

Matt. 11:29-30 Take My yoke upon you and learn from Me, for I am meek and lowly in heart, and you will find rest for your souls. For My yoke is easy and My burden is light.

1 Pet. 2:21 For to this you were called, because Christ also suffered on your behalf, leaving you a model so that you may follow in His steps.

Rom. 12:1 I exhort you therefore, brothers, through the compassions of God to present your bodies a living sacrifice, holy, well pleasing to God, which is your reasonable service.

Week 3 — Day 3 — Today's verses

Matt. 11:27 All things have been delivered to Me by My Father, and no one fully knows the Son except the Father; neither does anyone fully know the Father except the Son and him to whom the Son wills to reveal Him.

16:16-17 And Simon Peter answered and said, You are the Christ, the Son of the living God. And Jesus answered and said to him, Blessed are you, Simon Barjona, because flesh and blood has not revealed this to you, but My Father who is in the heavens.

Phil. 3:10 To know Him and the power of His resurrection and the fellowship of His sufferings, being conformed to His death.

Week 3 — Day 5 — Today's verses

Matt. 11:28-29 Come to Me all who toil and are burdened, and I will give you rest. Take My yoke upon you and learn from Me, for I am meek and lowly in heart, and you will find rest for your souls.

John 12:24 Truly, truly, I say to you, Unless the grain of wheat falls into the ground and dies, it abides alone; but if it dies, it bears much fruit.

Matt. 26:39 And going forward a little, He fell on His face and prayed, saying, My Father, if it is possible, let this cup pass from Me; yet not as I will, but as You will.

Week 3 — Day 2 — Today's verses

1 Cor. 1:26 For consider your calling, brothers, that there are not many wise according to flesh, not many powerful, not many wellborn.

Matt. 19:14 But Jesus said, Allow the little children and do not prevent them from coming to Me, for of such is the kingdom of the heavens.

Col. 1:26-27 The mystery which has been hidden from the ages and from the generations but now has been manifested to His saints; to whom God willed to make known what are the riches of the glory of this mystery among the Gentiles, which is Christ in you, the hope of glory.

Week 3 — Day 4 — Today's verses

Col. 1:17-18 And He is before all things, and all things cohere in Him; and He is the Head of the Body, the church; He is the beginning, the Firstborn from the dead, that He Himself might have the first place in all things.

Rev. 1:4 John to the seven churches which are in Asia: Grace to you and peace from Him who is and who was and who is coming, and from the seven Spirits who are before His throne.

John 17:6 I have manifested Your name to the men whom You gave Me out of the world. They were Yours, and You gave them to Me, and they have kept Your word.

Week 3 — Day 1 — Today's verses

Matt. 11:25-27 At that time Jesus answered and said, I extol You, Father, Lord of heaven and of earth, because You have hidden these things from the wise and intelligent and have revealed them to infants. Yes, Father, for thus it has been well-pleasing in Your sight. All things have been delivered to Me by My Father, and no one fully knows the Son except the Father; neither does anyone fully know the Father except the Son and him to whom the Son wills to reveal Him.

Week 4 — Day 1

Today's verses

Matt. 11:29 Take My yoke upon you and learn from Me, for I am meek and lowly in heart, and you will find rest for your souls.

14:19 And after commanding the crowds to recline on the grass, He took the five loaves and the two fish, and looking up to heaven, He blessed and broke the loaves and gave *them* to the disciples, and the disciples to the crowds.

_____
Date

Week 4 — Day 2

Today's verses

John 5:19 Then Jesus answered and said to them, Truly, truly, I say to you, The Son can do nothing from Himself except what He sees the Father doing, for whatever that One does, these things the Son also does in like manner.

10:30 I and the Father are one.

1 Cor. 2:3-4 And I was with you in weakness and in fear and in much trembling; and my speech and my proclamation were not in persuasive words of wisdom but in demonstration of the Spirit and of power.

_____
Date

Week 4 — Day 3

Today's verses

John 5:30 I can do nothing from Myself; as I hear, I judge, and My judgment is just, because I do not seek My own will but the will of Him who sent Me.

6:38 For I have come down from heaven not to do My own will but the will of Him who sent Me.

7:18 He who speaks from himself seeks his own glory; but He who seeks the glory of Him who sent Him, this One is true, and unrighteousness is not in Him.

_____
Date

Week 4 — Day 4

Today's verses

Matt. 14:22-23 And immediately He compelled the disciples to step into the boat and to go before Him to the other side, while He sent the crowds away. And after He sent the crowds away, He went up to the mountain privately to pray. And when night fell, He was there alone.

Luke 6:12 And in these days He went out to the mountain to pray, and He spent the whole night in prayer to God.

_____
Date

Week 4 — Day 5

Today's verses

Matt. 6:5-6 And when you pray, you shall not be like the hypocrites, because they love to pray standing in the synagogues and on the street corners, so that they may be seen by men. Truly I say to you, They have their reward in full. But you, when you pray, enter into your private room, and shut your door and pray to your Father who is in secret; and your Father who sees in secret will repay you.

13:6 But when the sun rose, they were scorched; and because they had no root, they withered.

_____
Date

Week 4 — Day 6

Today's verses

Exo. 33:11 And Jehovah would speak to Moses face to face, just as a man speaks to his companion......

John 6:27 Work not for the food which perishes, but for the food which abides unto eternal life, which the Son of Man will give you; for Him has the Father, *even* God, sealed.

_____
Date

Week 5 — Day 6

Today's verses

Phil. 4:5-7 — Let your forbearance be known to all men. The Lord is near. In nothing be anxious, but in everything, by prayer and petition with thanksgiving, let your requests be made known to God; and the peace of God, which surpasses every *man's* understanding, will guard your hearts and your thoughts in Christ Jesus.

Date _____

Week 5 — Day 3

Today's verses

Phil. 3:10 — To know Him and the power of His resurrection and the fellowship of His sufferings, being conformed to His death.

Rom. 6:6 — Knowing this, that our old man has been crucified with *Him* in order that the body of sin might be annulled, that we should no longer serve sin as slaves.

1 Cor. 15:31 — I protest by the boasting in you, brothers, which I have in Christ Jesus our Lord, I die daily.

Date _____

Week 5 — Day 5

Today's verses

1 Thes. 5:17 — Unceasingly pray.

Rom. 10:12 — For there is no distinction between Jew and Greek, for the same Lord *is Lord* of all *and* rich to all who call upon Him.

13 — For "whoever calls upon the name of the Lord shall be saved."

Phil. 1:21 — For to me, to live is Christ...

Date _____

Week 5 — Day 2

Today's verses

1 Pet. 2:21 — For to this you were called, because Christ also suffered on your behalf, leaving you a model so that you may follow in His steps.

Matt. 16:24 — Then Jesus said to His disciples, If anyone wants to come after Me, let him deny himself and take up his cross and follow Me.

2 Cor. 5:15 — And He died for all that those who live may no longer live to themselves but to Him who died for them and has been raised.

Gal. 2:19 — For I through law have died to law that I might live to God.

Date _____

Week 5 — Day 4

Today's verses

Phil. 2:3-4 — *Doing* nothing by way of selfish ambition nor by way of vainglory, but in lowliness of mind considering one another more excellent than yourselves; not regarding each his own virtues, but each the virtues of others also.

21 — For all seek their own things, not the things of Christ Jesus.

3:3 — For we are the circumcision, the ones who serve by the Spirit of God and boast in Christ Jesus and have no confidence in the flesh.

Date _____

Week 5 — Day 1

Today's verses

Rom. 8:29 — Because those whom He foreknew, He also predestinated *to be* conformed to the image of His Son, that He might be the Firstborn among many brothers.

John 5:30 — I can do nothing from Myself; as I hear, I judge, and My judgment is just, because I do not seek My own will but the will of Him who sent Me.

14:9 — Jesus said to him, Have I been so long a time with you, and you have not known Me, Philip? He who has seen Me has seen the Father; how *is it that* you say, Show us the Father?

Date _____

Week 6 — Day 4   Today's verses

Col. We give thanks to God, the Father of our
1:3 Lord Jesus Christ, praying always
concerning you.

1 Cor. But he who is joined to the Lord is one
6:17 spirit.

2 Tim. The Lord be with your spirit. Grace be
4:22 with you.

_____
Date

Week 6 — Day 5   Today's verses

Col. Persevere in prayer, watching in it with
4:2 thanksgiving.

1 Tim. But the profane and old-womanish myths
4:7 refuse, and exercise yourself unto godliness.

Eph. By means of all prayer and petition, pray-
6:18 ing at every time in spirit and watching
unto this in all perseverance and petition
concerning all the saints.

_____
Date

Week 6 — Day 6   Today's verses

Col. If therefore you were raised together with
3:1-2 Christ, seek the things which are above,
where Christ is, sitting at the right hand
of God. Set your mind on the things
which are above, not on the things which
are on the earth.

4:3 Praying at the same time for us also, that
God would open to us a door for the
word, to speak the mystery of Christ (because of which also I am bound).

12 Epaphras, who is one of you, a slave of
Christ Jesus, greets you, always struggling
on your behalf in his prayers that you
may stand mature and fully assured in all
the will of God.

Week 6 — Day 1   Today's verses

Col. When Christ our life is manifested, then
3:4 you also will be manifested with Him in
glory.

Eph. That Christ may make His home in your
3:17 hearts through faith...

4:24 And put on the new man, which was
created according to God in righteousness and holiness of the reality.

_____
Date

Week 6 — Day 2   Today's verses

Col. Let no one therefore judge you in eating
2:16-17 and in drinking or in respect of a feast or
of a new moon or of the Sabbath, which
are a shadow of the things to come, but
the body is of Christ.

_____
Date

Week 6 — Day 3   Today's verses

Col. And have put on the new man, which is
3:10-11 being renewed unto full knowledge according to the image of Him who created
him, where there cannot be Greek and
Jew, circumcision and uncircumcision,
barbarian, Scythian, slave, free man, but
Christ is all and in all.

Eph. Being diligent to keep the oneness of the
4:3-4 Spirit in the uniting bond of peace: one
Body and one Spirit...

_____
Date